Foreword by Melville Bell Grosvenor, *Editor-in-Chief*,
National Geographic Society, *Washington, D. C.*
Melvin M. Payne, *President*
Gilbert M. Grosvenor, *Editor*

Veiled by early-morning mist, the "Father of Waters" meanders through wooded marshlands i

Mighty Mississippi

By Bern Keating   *Photographs by* James L. Stanfield

Prepared by the National Geographic Society's Special Publications Division,
Robert L. Breeden, *Chief*

northern Minnesota, beginning a restless journey of nearly 2,350 miles south to the Gulf of Mexico.

THE MIGHTY MISSISSIPPI
By BERN KEATING

Photographs by JAMES L. STANFIELD
National Geographic Photographer

Published by
THE NATIONAL GEOGRAPHIC SOCIETY
MELVIN M. PAYNE, *President*
MELVILLE BELL GROSVENOR, *Editor-in-Chief*
GILBERT M. GROSVENOR, *Editor*
ROBERT PAUL JORDAN, *Consulting Editor*
CHARLES R. KOLB, *Consultant,*
  Chief, Geology Branch, U. S. Army
  Engineer Waterways Experiment Station,
  Vicksburg, Mississippi
JOHN FRANCIS MCDERMOTT, *Consultant, Research*
  Professor, Southern Illinois University
  at Edwardsville

Prepared by
THE SPECIAL PUBLICATIONS DIVISION
ROBERT L. BREEDEN, *Editor*
DONALD J. CRUMP, *Associate Editor*
PHILIP B. SILCOTT, *Manuscript Editor*
TEE LOFTIN SNELL, *Research and Assistant to the*
  Editor
MARJORIE W. CLINE, MARGERY G. DUNN,
  Research

Illustrations
DAVID R. BRIDGE, *Picture Editor*
JOSEPH A. TANEY, *Staff Art Director*
JOSEPHINE B. BOLT, *Art Director*
URSULA PERRIN, *Design Assistant*
MARGERY G. DUNN, H. ROBERT
  MORRISON, GERALD S. SNYDER,
  Picture Legends
ANN H. CROUCH, *Picture Legend Research*
JOHN D. GARST, JR., MONICA T. WOODBRIDGE,
  ISKANDAR BADAY, *Map Research and Production*

Production and Printing
ROBERT W. MESSER, *Production Manager*
MARGARET M. SKEKEL, *Production Assistant*
JAMES R. WHITNEY, JOHN R. METCALFE,
  Engraving and Printing
TUCKER L. ETHERINGTON, SUZANNE J. JACOBSON,
  RAJA D. MURSHED, DONNA REY NAAME,
  JOAN PERRY, SUZANNE B. THOMPSON, *Staff*
  Assistants
JOLENE MCCOY, VIRGINIA S. THOMPSON, *Index*

Standard Book Number 87044-096-9
Library of Congress Catalog Card Number 70-151944

PAGE 1: COLLECTION OF LEONARD V. HUBER, NEW ORLEANS;
ENDPAPERS: RICHARD SCHLECHT; OVERLEAF AND RIGHT:
NATIONAL GEOGRAPHIC PHOTOGRAPHER JAMES L. STANFIELD

*Young girl steps cautiously across a bridge
of stones at Lake Itasca, Minnesota, source
of the Mississippi River. Page 1: Plantation workers carry cottonseed aboard the
steamboat* America. *Endpapers: Vast
Mississippi drainage basin, third largest
in the world, takes in more than 1,245,000
square miles in 31 states and two Canadian
provinces. Sunlight glints from the Gulf
of Mexico at the river's mouth. Book-
binding: Fisherman casts from a johnboat
on Alligator Bayou in the Louisiana delta.*

Foreword

W**ITH THE RIVER CURRENT** to aid our new diesels, we made real speed downstream. Suddenly we rounded a bend, and saw a spectacle from Mark Twain's day: perhaps a dozen old paddle-wheel steamers nosed into the embankment, loading wartime cargo.

This was March of 1944, and as naval correspondent for NATIONAL GEOGRAPHIC I was making a pre-D-Day report on our new amphibious fleet. At Neville Island near Pittsburgh, Pennsylvania, I had boarded a brand-new United States Navy LST (Landing Ship, Tank) to sail down the Ohio and Mississippi Rivers to the Gulf of Mexico. The trip turned into a most fascinating voyage, for the war had pressed all the old vessels into service. A veteran Mississippi pilot and skeleton ferry crew navigated while the green complement of LST 654 learned the ropes.

"Watch the current," the old pilot told us. "You'll find the channel where you see fast water. Go in close—almost bounce off the bank." Deftly, he steered an S-shaped course from one side to the other.

As we cruised out of the Ohio into the Mississippi, I thought about the thousand sources of that muddy water—from the canyons cutting Western prairies to the steep, coal-bearing mountains of the Monongahela. Here was a flowing summary of American geography and history.

Sometimes we would meet tugs and barges and stern-wheelers chugging slowly upstream, keeping to the inside of bends where current was less. In narrow passages we skinned past like trains, with little room to spare. Other craft saluted our new battle-bound ship with honking horns and shouts. Once we passed an old showboat, and just as quickly we raced by the lighted waterfront of Memphis one evening at dusk.

Like the stern-wheelers of the 19th century, we tied up along the bank every night and looked out at eye level onto riverside fields. Our farm boy bos'n talked crops and cattle to the people he met.

For much of the trip I read Mark Twain's *Life on the Mississippi*. I could easily imagine myself in the pilothouse of the *Aleck Scott* with Sam Clemens himself twirling the wheel. As we passed the bluff at Vicksburg, General Grant's own memoirs told the story of the fierce battles, the months of maneuvering, and the 47-day siege that split the Confederacy.

Beyond New Orleans, we moved past blossom-scented orange groves to Pilottown, Louisiana, near the spot where muddy fresh water meets the salty Gulf. There the ship's wartime crew at last took command of their LST 654 and sailed off to war.

And now in word and picture, the same Mississippi flows through these pages—carrying its unique cargo of fact and folkway. No river has played a greater role in the story of America. Good reading!

MELVILLE BELL GROSVENOR

Above Minnesota's Winnibigoshish Lake on the Mississippi River, fisherman James A. Kohel waits in comfort fo

Contents

...rthern pike and walleye to rise to the bait.

"JOLLY FLATBOATMEN IN PORT," GEORGE CALEB BINGHAM, 1857, CITY ART MUSEUM OF ST. LOUIS

To the lilt of a fiddle, the beat of knuckles on a skillet, the tap of jigging feet, and the slap of the Mississippi Riv

Rivulet to Brawling Giant

...gainst the wharf, 19th-century flatboatmen idle away the time before casting off from St. Louis.

*L*IKE MILLIONS of other American boys, I grew up enthralled by the stories and legends of the Mississippi River. I read avidly of titanic battles between rival keelboatmen in the stews of Natchez-Under-the-Hill, thundering clashes of Union gunboats and Confederate batteries on the heights of Vicksburg, great log drives along the river's first 500 miles, week-long poker games aboard dazzling stern-wheeler floating palaces, bloody duels on sandbars over affronts to honor, Indian wars on the high prairie banks of the upper river.

The difference between me and most of my contemporaries who reread *The Adventures of Huckleberry Finn* whenever daily routine palled lies in the great good luck that dropped me on the banks of the Mississippi immediately after World War II. Most of my adult life I have spent within sound of towboats bawling for passage around Walker Bend.

For a quarter of a century I watched my little river-port town of Greenville, Mississippi, grow from a tree-shaded cotton port to a bustling little city of 42,000 boasting a towboat-building industry that matches any other on the Mississippi system and a customs office handling shipments abroad. As a journalist I have been privileged to record some of the transformations that a skyrocketing economy and explosive social changes have worked along the river's banks.

In the lower river country I knew dozens of riverbank towns with moss-hung and tradition-haunted streets, a plantation home or two where the offer of a walking-horse mount and a stirrup cup are automatic, some islands in the stream where friends keep secret knowledge of red wolf packs that still survive, and the hedonistic hangouts of New Orleans.

Still, I asked myself, even after 25 years of listening to the lonely blasts of towboats, of hearing the calls of wild geese scudding low at night under dripping autumn skies down the Mississippi flyway, what did I really know of the rest of that vast river that flows nearly 2,350 miles from northern lake country to its delta in the Gulf of Mexico? The long reach of the river north of me I knew only from those songs and books that had colored my boyhood imagination with fantasies of high adventure, of roistering lumber towns, of steamboats billowing clouds of black smoke.

And yet I knew from statistics alone that such a picture now bears no resemblance to the Mississippi, central water highway for a funnel-shaped basin beginning in Canada and ultimately taking in all or part of 31 states that produce nearly 75 percent of our gross national product.

To find out about life along the river today, I wanted to visit the people who live on its banks, to hear their stories, and to join them at work and at play in their cities and towns, at their resorts and fishing grounds, and on their farms. And I would ride on the waters of the Mississippi to see the navigation and flood-control works built during the past 40 years to help control this giant, bringing prosperity and an unprecedented measure of security to its great valley.

Before I started my journey, I steeped myself in river lore, reading histories, geographies, geological studies, commerce reports, accounts of industrial and urban growth in mid-America. Although the Congo and the Amazon have larger drainage basins than the Mississippi, and 14 rivers are longer—including one of its own tributaries, the Missouri—no river basin matches the Mississippi's in productivity. Besides being one of the greatest food-producing areas in the world, the extreme lower river region has vast oil and gas fields, and deposits of salt and sulphur.

And five navigable tributaries—the Illinois, Missouri, Ohio, Arkansas, and Ouachita—along with several feeder streams, bring cargo from as far east as Pittsburgh, from Tulsa, Kansas City, Omaha, and Sioux City in the west, from Chicago in the north, and from upper Alabama in the south.

Some legends about the physical character of North America's greatest river stick resolutely in the minds even of people along its banks. Many, for example, consider it almost unpatriotic not to accept the Mississippi as the world's muddiest river—"too thick to drink and too thin to plow." True, the Mississippi carries 50 pounds of mud in each 1,000 cubic feet— about three cups of mud to ten thousand of water—but the Missouri and the lower Colorado each carries ten or more times as much solid burden.

Visitors often picture the lower river as riding between levees just high enough to hold the water in, on an elevated bed that rises a little every year. Because of that widespread belief, many fellow passengers on a trip I made aboard the stern-wheeler *Delta Queen* expected to be able to look down on riverside plantations. Actually, 30-foot-high levees loomed overhead, shutting off the view even from the Texas deck, highest sightseeing platform aboard that delightfully anachronistic vessel.

The river bottom is in fact always at least a few feet below the surrounding lowlands. From Baton Rouge to New Orleans, the deepest part of the river, it lies 40 to 100 feet down, and at bends the currents dig as deep as 200 feet. During floods, the Mississippi has been known to rise 25 feet above its banks. In times past, spreading floodwaters dropped most of the sediment close to the stream and formed natural levees that were 10 to 15 feet high when the first Europeans arrived in the 16th century.

Virtually everybody believes that the river, by dumping its tremendous load of silt into the Gulf, is building land farther and farther out into the deep sea as it has for uncounted centuries. But Dr. Sherwood M. Gagliano of the Coastal Studies Institute at Louisiana State University, Baton Rouge, told me: "The present mouth of the Mississippi lies close to the edge of the continental shelf, not at a good distance from it as in past eras when the river flowed down old channels farther west. At the present mouth, about 75 percent of the river's discharge reaches the edge of the shelf and most of the fine sediment cascades into the abyss. Coarser material stops on the shelf, but it takes a long, long time to build up a land mass through such deep water. However, in the shallows close to shore, the other 25 percent of the river's discharge has been caught, and the sediment dropped there has built the familiar birdfoot delta. The delta is still building in some places, but eroding in others. We're working on plans to catch in those shallows even more Mississippi sediment and increase the amount of our delta land. We're also trying to find ways to stop the alarming loss from subsidence and erosion of some 16 square miles a year of old river-built lands."

ACTS ABOUT THE Mississippi usually apply only to certain portions, for the river changes character several times. Beginning at Minnesota's Lake Itasca, it flows through swamps, lakes, and second-growth pine forests, and down small rapids and between rising banks to the Falls of St. Anthony at Minneapolis, dropping 700 feet in 513 miles, the steepest grade on the river. Occasional canoeists who navigate this stretch must portage around 12 dams. Along its banks much of the population is Chippewa Indian and Scandinavian.

From Minneapolis to Cairo, Illinois, the U. S. Army Corps of Engineers keeps the channel nine feet deep, enough for towboat and heavy barge navigation, with 29 dams and locks. Along this 856-mile stretch, high bluffs and rolling hills, wild wetlands and neat prairie farms, and more than 500 forested islands make magnificent scenery. Industry flourishes in towns crowning many high points overlooking the river. On many roadside mailboxes names are German and Scandinavian.

Just 17 miles above St. Louis, the Missouri joins the Mississippi, and for miles the two streams refuse to mix, the steel-gray Mississippi hugging the east bank and the chocolate-brown Missouri squeezing down the west.

At Cairo, Illinois, however, the broad Ohio River pours in, and from there south the Mississippi becomes the brawling giant of legend, flowing nearly a thousand miles in great loops through its wide, fertile valley. Writhing around bends, it eats away banks here, fills channels there, and gradually shifts about in its 15-mile-wide meander belt. In the past the river often cut across the narrow neck of one of its loops, an occurrence now rare because of man's stabilization efforts.

Between Cairo and Baton Rouge names are mostly Anglo-Saxon, though many a Smith and Montgomery, Hinds and Cunningham has a black face. For these fertile bottomlands were cleared for cotton, sugarcane, and rice by white planters and an army of transplanted, enslaved Africans.

From Baton Rouge to below New Orleans names are mostly French. The Gallic quality of that stretch of the river is a reflection of the French power that once dominated the entire valley, for the story of the river's exploration and early settlement, after one major exception at the outset, became a French story.

That exception was the arrival at a flood-swollen Mississippi about halfway between present-day Memphis and Greenville, Mississippi, on May 8, 1541, of a lean and unkempt army of perhaps 400 Spanish conquistadors under Hernando de Soto, first Europeans to lay eyes on the stream.

They built rafts to cross the flood and wandered as far west as present-day Hot Springs, Arkansas. After they returned to the river, De Soto died, probably of malaria, and was slipped under the waters at night to keep hostile Indians from knowing the man they feared was gone. The surviving conquistadors ultimately paddled and floated down the river in seven unwieldy pinnaces, fighting Indians and mosquitoes 700 miles to the Gulf.

No white man ventured near the great stream again for 132 years, but rumors of its existence reached the French as they spread westward from Montreal along the Great Lakes.

Hoping the river would slice across the continent to the western sea and give France a shortcut to the East Indies, the governor of New France cast about for explorers to seek that fabled Northwest Passage. He asked Louis Jolliet, a fur trader, and Father Jacques Marquette, a Jesuit missionary, to find the outlet of the Messipi, the "big river" of the Chippewas. With five voyageurs in May 1673 they paddled and portaged two canoes from the Great Lakes to the Wisconsin River and traveled it to the Mississippi. At present-day Prairie du Chien, they headed south on the big river.

When the explorers had ventured as far as the St. Francis River in what is now Arkansas, they realized the Messipi was not cutting through to the Pacific, but flowing steadily south. Uncertain whether Spaniards held the river farther down, they turned back on July 17.

Even before their return, a well-born French adventurer in Montreal named René Robert Cavelier, Sieur de La Salle, grasped the significance of a great central waterway down the middle of the continent and conceived a brilliant scheme of empire. He planned a chain of forts and trading posts the length of the river to dominate the fur trade of the continent's interior. La Salle engaged a one-handed Italian soldier of fortune, Henri de Tonti, as his lieutenant and set out in December 1681 with a party of 23 Frenchmen, 28 Indian men and women, and three children. He reached the Gulf in a fleet of canoes in April 1682 without seeing a single Spaniard. At the mouth he raised a column and a cross, claiming the entire Mississippi Valley for France and naming it Louisiana for his King, Louis XIV.

Five years later, La Salle tried to find the river's mouth from the sea but missed it and ended up on the coast of Texas, where some of his own men murdered him during a disastrous attempt to establish a colony. Tonti, his leader dead, set up the chain of forts and ran them until his own government closed them near the turn of the century. The river was left to a few French trappers and traders. After 1718 they used as a capital and seaport near the river's mouth a new village in the canebrakes called New Orleans.

France ceded its Mississippi lands to Spain in 1763. During the 1790's, Americans were excluded from sending cargoes downriver, but then restrictions were relaxed, and trade and immigration surged forward. In 1802 Spain again closed New Orleans to the Americans, just as Napoleon prepared to send troops to repossess the whole of the territory. The western settlers became alarmed and angered. "The Mississippi is to them every-thing," wrote the Governor of Kentucky to President Thomas Jefferson. "It is the Hudson, the Delaware, the Potomac, and all the navigable rivers of the Atlantic states, formed into one stream." Jefferson's ministers set out to buy New Orleans, and Napoleon sold the entire Louisiana Territory. The fledgling United States took possession in 1803. North of Baton Rouge only a few place-names—La Crosse, Prairie du Chien, St. Louis, Ste. Genevieve—remain to mark the presence of the French, who once laid claim to all mid-America.

After the Louisiana Purchase, American settlers swarming westward into new lands along the waterway sent downstream the produce that burst from their fertile farms: tobacco, flour, furs, wheat, corn, whiskey. New Orleans in 1817 welcomed hundreds of rafts, flatboats, and keelboats.

By brute muscle power, barge and keelboat men moved their expensive craft home against the current, bringing mostly sugar, molasses, and gro-ceries. Sometimes they poled or paddled; sometimes they sailed or dragged their craft with ropes from shore. From New Orleans to Pittsburgh took four months or more, depending on luck and skill in dealing with storms, sandbars, snags, low or flood-stage currents, and Indian attacks. Keelers were tough, and they brawled and drank at stops like Natchez as if each day might be their last on what they called "the wicked river."

IN 1811 Nicholas Roosevelt—a distant relative of the Presidents— took the *New Orleans,* a 116-foot-long side-wheeler steamboat, from Pittsburgh to New Orleans, stopping at river ports along the way to demonstrate his vessel's ability to travel upstream against the current, and inaugurated the most colorful period in the river's history.

The boat immediately went into service on the New Orleans-Natchez run, but within two years it hit a stump and sank. During the whole of their era, steamboats rarely lasted more than five years. By 1849 snags, collisions, fires, groundings, and explosions of poorly tended boilers had sent 520 of them to the bottom. But profits ran high and in that same year 600 steam packets worked the river despite all hazards.

The Civil War and the mushroom growth of railroads killed the steam-boat era. Trains traveled faster and they traveled year-round, while pack-ets, increasingly bigger and heavier, had to stop running when the river was too low to float them. By 1910 steamboat cargo tonnage handled at St. Louis had dropped to 10 percent of peak periods half a century earlier.

About the same year, a fleet of ten Government-operated dredges finished digging a channel nine feet deep at low water from Cairo to the Head of Passes at the Mississippi's mouth. Once again the big packets began steaming up and down the river, pushing their cargo on long platforms of barges lashed together.

During World War I, a Government desperate for more transport created the Federal Barge Lines, later sold to private owners. By 1931 river freight had doubled the biggest year of the steam-packet century.

Transport needs of World War II gave the river another powerful stimulus with extraordinary cargoes built at inland ports and carried to sea by the river. I watched, for example, my own destroyer-escort, the U.S.S. *Raby*, built in Bay City, Michigan, pass under the bridge at Greenville on her way to New Orleans. Soon I would board her for 20 months of Pacific duty, during which she would take part in the sinking of six submarines.

Between 1958 and 1968 river cargo almost doubled, to 219 million tons, and is expected to double again in the next decade. Revolutionary concepts of hoisting loaded river barges and giant cargo containers aboard seagoing vessels by crane may cause an explosive growth of river traffic.

Since the 1940's the Corps of Engineers has been committed by Congress to maintain a 40-foot depth to Baton Rouge and 12 feet to Vicksburg, as well as keep open the 9-foot channel to the Falls of St. Anthony.

To reduce bank caving, particularly where the river chews savagely at its bends, engineers have laid acres of articulated concrete mats. They have built jetties, or long walls, out from shore to force currents into midstream for scouring out the channel. And they have sliced across 15 looping bends to shorten the river and speed the flow.

But the river keeps gnawing away and the engineers keep fighting back in an endless struggle.

Every few years great blizzards carpet the upper drainage basin, a freakish spring thaw melts the snow but not the frozen earth, spring rains drop unprecedented loads for upland tributaries to drain off, and a prodigious flood heads downstream.

In 1927 floodwaters drove more than 600,000 people from their homes in the lower river floodplain; in places water ran 80 miles wide. The major levee failure happened just north of Greenville, and to this day old-timers measure history as "befo' '27" and "aftuh '27," for they spent weeks going about their business by poling johnboats. My wife dimly recalls helping her weeping mother carry belongings to the attic of their house in McGehee, Arkansas. There they awaited rescue for a week while living on cold canned beans and peanut butter.

After that disaster, Congress authorized the Corps to build a flood-control system for the lower river. To drain off great volumes of water at critical points, floodways were built between Cairo, Illinois, and New Madrid, Missouri; in the Atchafalaya Basin; and at Morganza above Baton Rouge. At New Orleans a spillway diverts floodwaters to the sea through

Lake Pontchartrain. To protect land and people along the river, the engineers built nearly 1,600 miles of levees 15 to 40 feet high on lowlands from Cape Girardeau, Missouri, to below New Orleans.

In 1937 floodwaters approaching those of 1927 in volume tested the new levee system. At Arkansas City, Arkansas, as a college student on vacation I helped volunteers stack sandbags around geysers of water that had tunneled under the earthworks. When the sandbag chimneys reached the height of the river lapping against the other side of the levee, pressures stabilized and the "boil" was contained. The levees passed the test without a failure, for the builders meant them to withstand a superflood at least 20 percent greater than the 1927 ordeal.

Still, when I stand on the familiar banks of the lower river at high water and watch great oaks whirl dizzyingly around a swirling vortex trying to suck them to the bottom, when I see an acre of forested land collapse and slide, trees and all, into the hungry river, I leave the scene with an uneasy awe for the blind power of an almost supernatural force.

My reading and library research done, I immersed myself in the undeniable magic of that immense river, planting my feet on the Mississippi mud the length of the stream. During six months, I traveled on foot and horseback, by helicopter, fishing skiff, towboat, jeep, and swamp buggy. I doubled back to take in festivals, sporting matches, harvests, hunting, trapping, and logging seasons, boat races, events that make the banks of the mighty Mississippi by turns backwoods and cosmopolitan, wilderness and metropolitan, moribund and bustling.

I began the trip at the obvious place, at the official source of the river itself, a starting point that delayed an astonishing time in entering history. The navigable stretches of the river carried a booming steamboat traffic from St. Paul to the sea for years before the source was discovered. Army expeditions explored the misty fens of the northland in fruitless efforts. Then, in 1832, Henry Schoolcraft, an Indian agent, had the good sense to ask local Indians where the stream started. Following the Chippewa guide Ozawindeb (Yellowhead), Schoolcraft reached a Y-shaped pool, called Elk Lake by the Indians and voyageurs, and renamed it Itasca, a name he confected out of the central syllables of the Latin words *veritas* and *caput* to signify "true head."

When I reached Itasca, in the lake country of Minnesota 120 miles south of the Canadian border, I found tourists gathered almost elbow to elbow, gazing at a Mississippi only 20 feet wide and six inches deep at normal water level. Rangers have made a bridge of stones, but most visitors prefer to wade the river and splash about joyously.

Suddenly, summer storm clouds boiled over a low ridge, part of the watershed that turns the Mississippi from a course that otherwise would lead it to Hudson Bay. Sheets of rain swept the lake. The tourists ran to the shelter of their automobiles, but I held firm. Ankle-deep in the rushing waters, I watched the stream, swollen by rain, creep perceptibly up my legs. For at the source of the Mississippi River, a rainstorm wetting only a few square miles can cause a lilliputian flash flood. As a river dweller where high-water crests can run a mile and three-quarters wide, I wanted to experience that tiny crest at Lake Itasca so I could tell the skeptical folk back home. As soon as the sky cleared, I tried walking downstream to find the first house on the Mississippi. Within a few steps I realized why foot traffic is light—nonexistent actually—along the river's extreme upper reaches. After leaving the lake, those shower-freshened waters trickled northeast some 40 miles through willows and marsh grasses that concealed the stream and its borders. In many places I could not tell if a river flowed or if I was merely slogging across a sodden marsh. Hordes of mosquitoes attacked me. The only animal life I saw was a porcupine girdling a magnificent red pine, and a cete of badgers—strayed from their prairie home 30 miles to the west—waddling lost across a spongy meadow.

The first house, about three-fourths of a mile downstream, carried the sign "Headwaters Inn," and there kindly Ruth Starbuck, the proprietress, provided me with a sandwich and a chilled bottle of beer.

Up to this "first resort on the Mississippi River," the stream affords only a shallow canoe trail. I took to the highway, driving to the Bemidji area before coming to a complex of resorts based on truly boatable water. This is Paul Bunyan country. The town's 18-foot statue of the fabled lumberman, with his great blue ox Babe, and a re-created logging camp nearby, remind visitors of the 50 years or so in the 19th and early 20th centuries when the surrounding pine forests were cut and floated to sawmills downstream. Now more than 100,000 campers and water and winter sports enthusiasts come each year to the area's hundreds of wilderness lakes. At "Kohl's Last Resort" on Big Turtle Lake north of town I found the proprietor building an addition to his lodge.

Once a free-lance commercial photographer in Chicago, Robert B. Kohl had abandoned the "rat race" shortly after World War II and moved to the North Woods. A hard outdoor life had made his 6-foot-4 frame muscular and spare, and he swung great slabs of insulation board into place with ease. I expressed amazement at his strength.

"It's just styrofoam," he said. "A toddler could balance a piece as big as a dance floor on his head. But it's the big breakthrough in the winterizing business. Winter here brings temperatures down as low as 50 below zero with three to four feet of snow on the ground for five months. Styrofoam is so cheap and efficient I can build this addition without borrowing much money and rush to get ready for the snowmobilers who'll begin arriving in mid-November."

I knew of the mounting excitement over the revolution that the snowmobile, introduced in the early 1960's, was making in winter recreation. On the radio, I had heard that Minnesota had licensed 114,646 snowmobiles by mid-August of 1970. And dealers had predicted they would sell almost half again that many before deep winter in December. Northern

Minnesota manufacturers make 60 percent of the snowmobiles turned out in the United States and almost 20 percent of the world's production.

"What do snowmobiles mean to the northern resort owner? They mean year-round work and income," Bob said. "Minnesota resorts used to open only for parts of July and August. You can't make a decent living working two months a year. But industry is beginning to stagger vacations the year round, schools are going to the trimester system and releasing the kids for winter vacations, and the snowmobile is giving the whole family all outdoors to play in.

"Except for the occasional ice-fishing fan, we used to hole up during the winter and slowly get 'cabin fever.' Now, on the first snowy weekend, vacationers come up and rent 'his' and 'her' snowmobiles for $7.50 an hour each, pop the kids on the back seats, and drive off in their motorized sleds for an all-day run over wilderness trails."

But snowmobiles are not without hazards. They cruise at about 60 miles an hour and in the hands of reckless or inexperienced drivers have been in serious accidents. They have rammed into trees, or overturned when their drivers tried to jump them from a drift to a lower level. And studies are under way to determine if they have caused some disturbance to wildlife, particularly deer and grouse.

Virtually all states and Canadian provinces require licensing and driver training, and limit snowmobiles to rural areas. Minnesota's statutes and driver-training programs in public schools have become models. Violators who drive down forbidden roadways or across posted lands soon learn that sheriff's deputies and game wardens have even faster snowmobiles — and a heavy hand at writing tickets.

OWNSTREAM FROM Bemidji for a hundred miles the Mississippi runs east and strings together a chain of azure lakes. Most of the land is only marginally fertile and forested by second-growth pine, source of a still-vigorous logging and pulpwood industry.

In hamlets along the road almost as far as Brainerd, 75 miles south of Grand Rapids, I saw as much copper skin as white, for the riverside highway runs through Chippewa lands. The Chippewas came from the east in the 18th century and fought savage battles with the Sioux over the lakes and their crops of wild rice. With French firearms received as trade goods for their furs the Chippewas crushed their enemies, still armed with Stone Age weapons, and drove them to the Great Plains.

The wild rice in shallow lakes visible from the highway was ripening when I drove into Grand Rapids — where the Mississippi turns south, deflected by a slight elevation that stops it from running into Lake Superior and the Atlantic Ocean. I sought out Clifton E. Nelson, who dominates trading in the grain along the headwaters. A stocky 40-year-old Swede who has invented and hand-constructed the roasters and hullers he uses to process the harvest, Cliff explained to me the economics of the business, about to be revolutionized by the expanding cultivation of wild rice. Curiously, for the tycoon of an enterprise that demands aggressiveness at Indian auctions and iron nerves during price gyrations on the big-city markets, Cliff speaks in a soft and diffident manner. He had to invite me twice to visit some cultivated paddies before I understood him.

A few miles west of Grand Rapids, we met Mert Lego, a part-Indian farmer, in his paddies on the banks of the Mississippi. Mert gazed with obvious satisfaction over two fields totaling 100 acres almost ready to harvest. To the eye, the grains of his cultivated *Zizania aquatica* — botanically unrelated to *Oryza sativa*, the domestic rice of ordinary commerce — look exactly like the wild grains growing in nearby lakes. "And they taste exactly alike," Mert said. "Even the ducks can't tell the difference."

Flocks of mallards, teal, widgeons, shovelers, and pairs of wood ducks streaked low across the fields, often plunging into the paddy. I speculated on the great hunting Mert could expect on the season's opening day. He looked horrified.

"Nobody lays a finger on those ducks," he said. "They help solve my biggest problem in raising wild rice. The grains ripen from the top down and most fall to the ground, so we harvest only about 300 pounds of the 900 that grow on each acre. We hope the ducks will scoop up the bulk of the 600 pounds that fall and leave just the right seeding from the handful they overlook. Only 40 pounds of seed to the acre make a good crop. Any denser seeding turns out spindly, weak, low-yielding rice."

But what about the Indians, I asked. Didn't they have a monopoly from the Government on wild rice harvest? Wouldn't they protest cultivation of wild rice?

"They have control over who goes ricing on their reservations, and they have the exclusive privilege of ricing on some Government property, but there are rice beds that people who aren't Indians can harvest." Cliff said. "As for cultivated paddies, they're about to get out their war drums. You'll find out when you go ricing with the Chippewas."

On the Rice Lake National Wildlife Refuge, some 60 miles south of Grand Rapids, I set off in an outboard canoe to find the Indian harvesters. I ran aground repeatedly in the shallow lake, and in pushing off I got some idea of the brutal work demanded for a full day's ricing. Indians can make at least $100 each day of the two-week harvest, but they earn every dime, struggling through those shallows in bone-chilling September wind.

As I crossed the lake, I scared up vast numbers of migrating mallards and ringnecks feeding on the seed heads of wild celery poking above the surface. Near the farther shore I stopped alongside Alex Moose standing in the bow of his canoe, poling it through rice beds. His 29-year-old daughter Brenda was bending the grain over the gunwale with a stick about two feet long and with another "knocker" was lightly flailing the heads so that only the ripened grain fell into the boat.

Alex, a powerfully built man of 65, has the noble head of the Indian on a buffalo nickel. Graciously he interrupted the lucrative work of gathering a crop that brings him a penny for each small handful of kernels. He expanded his stately monologue from ricing to the decline of the Chippewa language among the young, citing a recent visit to Canada, where Indian youngsters spoke what he considered a barbarous dialect.

When I questioned Brenda, she gave me the same sad answer I have heard everywhere in North America among the children of those who speak minority languages. Like Cajun, Seneca, Athapascan, and Eskimo she replied, "I can understand it a little, but I don't speak much."

That afternoon in a warehouse on the lake shore, the tribe's auctioneer, Jerry Martin, chanted mounting prices and sold the day's gathering for $1.43 a pound. The average load for 35 canoes that day came to 98 pounds. During the season, a hard-working Indian harvester can bring in about a dozen loads in all.

I asked Alex and Sam Yankee, member at large of the Interior Department's Advisory Committee on Sport Fisheries and Wildlife, how they felt about the cultivation of wild rice. They glowered and protested and said that Indian delegations were trying to have Federal agencies forbid its sale under that name. But that same day's paper carried a story that a tribal cooperative, including Chippewas at Odanah, Wisconsin, had put in a pilot project of 100 acres to test the feasibility of growing wild rice on 2,000 acres of cultivated paddies.

From Brainerd I drove south through a more developed area of sandy farms, pine forests, and parklands. One park, named for Charles A. Lindbergh, preserves the house near Little Falls where the "Lone Eagle" grew up. A few miles north of St. Cloud the Mississippi funneled through a small gorge, prelude to the great river bluffs below Minneapolis. In roadside fields rows of sprinklers irrigated truck crops.

Soon I glimpsed St. Cloud, maker of optical lenses, railroad cars, boats, playground equipment, brooms, and neon signs. But the place is best known as "Granite City," for it quarries a fine-grained stone that ranges in hue from black through shades of red and pink to a clear white.

Between St. Cloud and the Twin Cities of Minneapolis-St. Paul, where the Mississippi changes from a minor stream to a major river, the highway is caught up in a tangle of expressways wrapped around the cities like the serpents around Laocoön and his sons.

Retired lumberjack Warren J. Huffman lounges on a buffalo hide from his own small herd. Antlers of elk and moose he once hunted for food decorate his log cabin near Pine River, Minnesota. The bear trap recalls its former owner—an old friend now dead.

On a summer morning some 15,000 years ago, caribou and mammoths graze on tender shoots of grass. Beyond them, in present-day Minnesota, looms a receding edge of the last of four ice sheets that covered the northern United States and Canada. Some geologists believe tundra carpeted the southern fringe of the ice, with plants growing on accumulated debris. Rock flour, silt from boulders ground by the ice, tinted the meltwater

lake murky white. The tremendous runoff from the glacier carried silt and sand down the Mississippi trench, partly filling its depths. Wind picked up sediment from the floodplain, dropping the sand nearby to form dunes and spreading finer material along the bordering uplands as loess. Today the mighty Mississippi, much smaller than the glacial runoff, winds through the ancient river bed atop post-glacial deposits.

"MIDNIGHT MASS ON THE MISSISSIPPI OVER THE BODY OF FERDINAND (SIC) DE SOTO, 1542,"
EDWARD MORAN, C. 1898, UNITED STATES NAVAL ACADEMY MUSEUM, ANNAPOLIS, MARYLAND

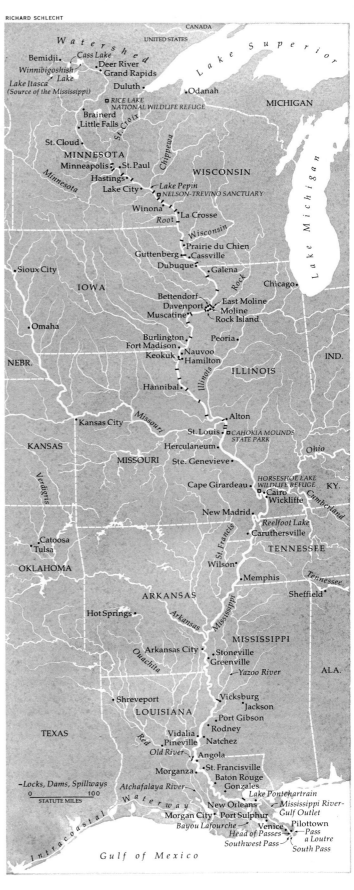

Watershed

CANADA
UNITED STATES

Lake Superior

Bemidji · Cass Lake
Winnibigoshish · Deer River
Lake · Grand Rapids
Lake Itasca
(Source of the Mississippi) · Duluth

· Odanah

MICHIGAN

☐ RICE LAKE
NATIONAL WILDLIFE REFUGE

Brainerd
Little Falls

St. Croix

St. Cloud ·

MINNESOTA
Minneapolis · · St. Paul
Hastings ·
Lake City ·

Chippewa

WISCONSIN

Lake Pepin
NELSON-TREVINO SANCTUARY

Winona
Root · La Crosse

Wisconsin

· Prairie du Chien
Guttenberg · · Cassville
Dubuque ·
· Galena

Rock

Chicago ·

· Sioux City

IOWA

Bettendorf ·
Davenport · · East Moline
Muscatine · · Moline
· Rock Island

Peoria ·

· Omaha

Burlington ·
Fort Madison ·
Keokuk · · Nauvoo
· Hamilton

Illinois

ILLINOIS

IND.

NEBR.

Hannibal ·

· Alton

· Kansas City

Missouri

St. Louis · ☐ CAHOKIA MOUNDS
STATE PARK

KANSAS

Herculaneum ·

MISSOURI
Ste. Genevieve ·

Ohio

Cape Girardeau · HORSESHOE LAKE
WILDLIFE REFUGE
· Cairo
· Wickliffe

KY.

Cumberland

New Madrid ·

Reelfoot Lake
· Caruthersville

Verdigris

· Catoosa
Tulsa ·

OKLAHOMA

St. Francis

Wilson ·

TENNESSEE

· Memphis

Tennessee

Sheffield ·

ARKANSAS

Hot Springs ·

Arkansas

Mississippi

MISSISSIPPI

Arkansas City ·
· Stoneville
· Greenville
· *Yazoo River*

Ouachita

ALA.

· Shreveport

· Vicksburg
· Jackson

LOUISIANA

· Port Gibson
· Rodney

Vidalia · · Natchez
Pineville ·
Old River · Angola

· St. Francisville
Morganza · · Baton Rouge
· Gonzales

TEXAS

Red

–Locks, Dams, Spillways
0   100
STATUTE MILES

Atchafalaya River–

Waterway

Lake Pontchartrain
New Orleans · · *Mississippi River-*
Morgan City · Port Sulphur · *Gulf Outlet*
Bayou Lafourche · · Venice · Pilottown
Head of Passes · *Pass
Southwest Pass · a Loutre
South Pass*

Intracoastal

Gulf of Mexico

Lake Michigan

René Robert Cavelier, Sieur de La Salle, greets Taensa Indians (above) in present-day Louisiana while exploring the Mississippi Valley. On April 9, 1682, he stood at the river's mouth and claimed its basin (partial map at right) for France. Almost a century and a half earlier, in 1541, Spanish explorer Hernando de Soto had discovered the river. A year later it became his grave. Comrades held the Mass at night to keep his death secret from hostile Indians, who feared him.

Showers of sparks stream from the stacks of Morning Star *and* Queen of the West *in a fanciful lithograph that captures the excitement of a steamboat race. Such exploits helped shorten a boat's life to an average of less than five years. At left, the* Mississippi *lies abandoned. Captain Thomas Paul Leathers (far right) lost a storied contest when the* Robert E. Lee *proved faster than his* Natchez *in 1870. His daughter-in-law, Captain Blanche Douglass Leathers (opposite, left), one of the few women who operated steamboats on the Mississippi, renewed her license until she died in 1940.*

CURRIER & IVES LITHOGRAPH, HARRY T. PETERS COLLECTION, MUSEUM OF THE CITY OF NEW YORK (BELOW); COLLECTION OF LEONARD V. HUBER, NEW ORLEANS (BOTH ABOVE)

Their floating housetop an uncertain refuge, a family clings to trust in God. In 1927,
eight years before John Steuart Curry painted this picture, heavy winter and spring
rains caused the worst flood in the history of the lower river. It inundated 26,000
square miles of the valley, killing some 200 people and leaving about 600,000 homeless.

Source of the Mississippi: Trickle of water escapes icebound Lake Itasca. Gurgling around snow-mantled stepping-stones, the stream heads northeast. By the time it reaches Bemidji, Minnesota, it has turned east, beginning the big swing south toward the Gulf of Mexico. Explorer Henry Schoolcraft discovered the source in 1832, and derived its name from the central syllables of veritas *and* caput, *Latin words chosen by Schoolcraft to designate the "true head." Established in 1891, Itasca State Park preserves about 50 square miles of woodlands around the lake. In spring, the marsh marigold (opposite at right) nods near its shores, and the wailing cry of the common loon (below) mingles with the hoarse croak of the leopard frog.*

COMMON LOON (GAVIA IMMER); LEOPARD FROG (RANA PIPIENS); MARSH MARIGOLD (CALTHA ILLUSTRIS)

Minnesotans along the Mississippi reap a varied bounty: Dipping suckers out of a net, fishermen near Bemidji strip eggs and milt into washtubs before releasing the fish. Fry hatched from the eggs will grow to bait size in ponds. At Grand Rapids, top loader David Root (far left) leans on his pickaroon, a hook-tipped pole he uses to stack pulpwood. Chippewa tribesman James Jackson harvests wild rice near Ball Club; son James, Jr., poles their boat. At right, Katherine Maras Matonich pauses in her vegetable garden at Hibbing, her home since 1913.

Recapturing the flavor of old-time showboats, the cast of Mississippi Melodie *at Grand Rapids, Minnesota, performs on a riverside stage. Engine screaming, a Formula A racer speeds down the straightaway at a track outside Brainerd. Chippewa children near Cass Lake swing high at recess.*

Golden torrent at Minnesota's Twin Cities pours from a grain elevator into a barge bound downriver. First major po

the Mississippi, Minneapolis and St. Paul ship more than 160 million bushels of grain annually.

*S*TEAMBOATS began puffing upstream from St. Louis a century and a half ago. During the next 50 years, they called at booming lead-mine towns, army posts, sawmill settlements, fur-trading villages, and jumping-off landings where tens of thousands of pioneers, including German and Scandinavian immigrants, pushed into the interior to find land on the prairies. With daring and skill pilots challenged both deadly flood and the hazards of low water to negotiate channels twisting among myriad islands. But they stopped cold below the Falls of St. Anthony, which began as a 16-foot cascade and frothed and tumbled another 60 feet in a seven-mile stretch. Further navigation upstream depended on portaged canoes and a few steamboats docked above the falls.

On high west-bank bluffs below the cascade, where the Minnesota River flows into the Mississippi, stood Fort Snelling, an outpost established in Indian territory in 1819. Soldiers and a few settlers hitched sawmill and gristmill to the racing water. In the late 1830's other settlers built a scattering of cabins on the east bank a few miles farther downstream on land purchased from the Sioux, at the head of practical steamboat navigation.

A French-Canadian trader nicknamed Pig's Eye did a lively business in the new settlement selling whiskey to the soldiers, and gave his name to the shantytown that sprang up around him when squatters at Fort Snelling were kicked out for selling whiskey to the Indians.

Later settlers of more sedate habits ultimately changed the name of the place to the less colorful but more respectable St. Paul.

In the 1850's land on the west bank beside the falls was opened to settlers, and a village called Minneapolis grew there, its name formed from the Sioux for "water" and the Greek for "city." Within 20 years it had enveloped hundreds of nearby lakes and swallowed, name and all, an older sawmill village called St. Anthony, ten miles upstream from St. Paul.

For decades hazardous steamboating on the upper Mississippi troubled pilots and settlers. Then in the early 1900's Congress directed the Corps of Engineers to pull out snags and boulders and create a channel six feet deep. That helped, but only in the past 30 years has the upper river become a reliable waterway with the construction of a system of locks and dams to provide a nine-foot channel. And cargo has increased from three million tons in 1939 to 49 million in 1969.

Together the Twin Cities, including their adjoining suburbs, number 1,814,000 people. Once the cities were described as standing back to back, for their citizens had an astonishing ability to ignore the existence of the rival community. But in the past ten years rivalry has greatly diminished. Now the cities take joint action on many projects. The Metropolitan Council, set up by the state legislature in 1967, works to coordinate area development, tackling such common problems and programs as land use, transportation, parks, pollution, and sewer and water systems.

Examples of intercity cooperation extend even to sports and music: The former Minneapolis Symphony Orchestra is now the Minnesota Symphony, supported by both cities; and Minneapolis and St. Paul share a single major-league baseball team, the Minnesota Twins. But the cities still have strongly individual personalities. I took in a superb stage performance at the world-famous Tyrone Guthrie Theater in Minneapolis and afterward met William E. McGivern, news director at KSTP-TV, to discuss the show and the differences in the two cities underlined by the audience's reaction. Bill assured me that the racy language calmly accepted by the Minneapolis audience would have drawn strong protests from a St. Paul crowd.

"The city line splits our office in two," he said, "and not by accident, for we broadcast and sell advertising to both audiences. So I think I can be objective—though I do live in St. Paul and wouldn't dream of moving.

"Minneapolis is banking, country-club sophistication, and pecking order; St. Paul is transportation, family gatherings, friendly squareness, and almost aggressive egalitarianism."

Attitudes obviously are changing, however. The controversial musical *Hair* came not to Minneapolis but to St. Paul, and the advance ticket sale totaled $250,000. Surprisingly, one of the strongest protests arose across the city limits—from a Minneapolis ministerial association.

Downtown Minneapolis, largely rebuilt in the 1960's, has more of a big-city look than St. Paul, which tore down its central 12 blocks only recently. But already the half-completed "Capital Center" is giving St. Paul a skyline as modern, if not as tall and imposing, as that of Minneapolis.

Like most of Minnesota—or indeed all of the Mississippi Valley from Dubuque, Iowa, north—the Twin Cities are heavily German and Scandinavian with a strong leavening of Irish in St. Paul, where mayors traditionally carry Irish names. But after 1965, when new U. S. immigration laws changed quotas to allow a much larger immigration from areas outside Europe, the makeup of the normal annual flow of about a thousand immigrants to the Twin Cities began to change. The hundreds of people coming from the Far East, Middle East, and Africa have begun to alter the Scandinavian-Celtic nature of the cities.

At the International Institute in St. Paul, an agency that helps newcomers adjust to life in the United States, executive director Robert J. Hoyle explained the changing immigration pattern in his city.

"In 1970 immigrants coming to St. Paul numbered 420, and almost half of them came from Asia and Africa. Most have a profession or skill, and they chose this area perhaps because it's a center of education and big industry.

"Unlike earlier immigrants, these newcomers do not form ethnic colonies but spread all over the city. That gives them a quick introduction to our culture, but deprives them of contact with their own. Many become terribly lonely, especially wives — who typically don't speak English. They truly despair if they have no friend to weep with them when word comes that a parent has died in the old country."

The growing cosmopolitanism of the Twin Cities came home to me at the 31st annual Aquatennial Celebration, a ten-day summer festival originally built around boating, skiing, and swimming contests held on the lakes and streams of Minneapolis. The show has expanded to include many nonwater events. On a mall decorated in Oriental style a beautiful Thai girl asked me for directions to the Thailand exhibit. Within three minutes, another Thai girl asked me the same question. By running after the first girl, I was able to introduce the countrywomen and they walked off arm-in-arm with one of them haltingly trying to speak a language she had almost forgotten in the New World.

The industrial giants based in the Twin Cities, like Minnesota Mining and Manufacturing, Honeywell, Control Data, and General Mills, still play an active part in solving local and national problems, but they grapple more and more with international concerns, a natural result of their extensive contact with foreign markets. The Twin Cities send abroad more than half a billion dollars' worth of goods yearly, ranking high among U. S. cities in exports. Products made at the Twin Cities range from Scotch tape to computers, truck axles to breakfast cereals, stuffed toys to tractor cabs, snowmobile suits to fabricated steel — and many are as familiar overseas as here at home.

Once interested almost exclusively in milling flour for the Nation's breakfast biscuits and other needs, General Mills now is taking a hard look at the food crises resulting from overpopulation in many nations of the world. At the company's James Ford Bell Technical Center research laboratories, I talked with Dr. A. D. Odell, Director of Special Programs. General Mills had just won the Kirkpatrick Achievement Award — something like a Nobel Prize in chemical engineering — for finding ways to convert soybean and other abundant vegetable proteins into palatable textured foods.

"Today," Dr. Odell told me, "much of the world's diet is deficient in quality protein, vitally needed for full physical and mental development. Serious health problems occur in many countries because meat, fish, eggs, or dairy products simply aren't available in quantity or are too expensive for most families.

"Our process, using soy or other oilseed protein fibers that are usually discarded, makes possible the creation of totally new foods, called analogs, that closely resemble meat in flavor, appearance, texture, and, most important, nutritional quality. Such protein is much less expensive than meat, and is being produced for restaurant use in the United States, mostly as frozen food. The same techniques we use could be applied to cottonseed

and peanut proteins in such countries as Pakistan and India, and feasibility studies for dried analogs are under way to help make this happen."

I know both Pakistan and India well and have seen the resistance there
to new foodstuffs. I expressed doubt that the people would accept a diet of
dried or reconstituted fibers, no matter how rich in protein.

"But therein lies the attraction of this soybean protein," Dr. Odell replied.
"We have learned in our laboratories how to give it any texture and flavor
to match any ethnic or religious bias."

As a parting present Dr. Odell gave me a kit of chunks and crumbles
variously labeled as chicken, beef, bacon, and seafood, and assured me his
chemists could as easily duplicate the taste of camel's hump or shark's fin.

ONE NONINTERNATIONAL CRISIS absorbs some of the residents of
the Twin Cities. As in most communities in the 1970's, citizens'
groups in Minneapolis-St. Paul question the impact on the environment of every new industrial project. Northern States Power Company had just proposed building, 40 miles upstream, a 680-megawatt
power plant burning some 9,600 tons of coal daily. I called on Arthur Dien-
hart, the power company's vice president in charge of engineering, to ask
what effect the plant would have on Minnesota's land, water, and air.

"About $15,000,000 of the construction cost will go for pollution-control
facilities," he said. "The plant is being designed to burn low-sulphur coal
from Montana because air-pollution agencies discourage the building of
new plants using high-sulphur coal from Illinois and Kentucky. For plants
already in operation, equipment is being tested to try to remove enough
sulphur to meet the new standards — and at economical cost. The design of
these old plants commits them to the continued use of coal with about
three percent sulphur. Western coal, with less than one percent sulphur,
will fuel the new plants."

Eugene A. Kraut, assistant executive vice president of the Port Authority
of St. Paul, confirmed the demand for coal from western fields.

"We're setting up for a steady flow of 100-car coal trains. Much of the fuel
will be used in this area, but dockside machines will pick up entire hopper
cars and dump their loads into barges to be pushed to new power plants
downstream and in the Ohio River Valley. In 1972 we expect three to four
million tons to move from the west through St. Paul, in addition to the
traditional 2½ million tons that flow from the south. I understand a town
in Kentucky near the Ohio River is named New Castle. Well, barges from
St. Paul are going to be carrying coal that way."

Next day I ventured downriver in an 18-foot fiberglass Crestliner boat
with Bob Farinacci and Jim Gove of the Division of Tourism of the State
of Minnesota Department of Economic Development. We passed below
200-foot bluffs where residential areas overlook the Mississippi. At bank
level some parks and recreational facilities have been provided, and

Eugene Kraut had told me that more were in the port authority's plans.

Oddly out of character in a state justifiably proud of its natural beauty, the river for a few miles below Minneapolis has a disturbingly scruffy look. Old factories, freight yards, tank farms, sand and gravel distribution firms, an abandoned packing plant, and refineries for oil from North Dakota and Canada clutter the banks.

From the Falls of St. Anthony to St. Louis, a distance of nearly 700 miles, the upper river descends 420 feet through a stepladder of narrow lakes ten to fifty miles long, each stored behind one of 29 dams. As river craft arrive at a dam, they enter a lock basin and wait until the water level is allowed to rise or fall to match the level of the next lake. Before the locks and dams were built, traffic almost came to a standstill during months of low water. Now continuous traffic is possible except in winter, when the river freezes shut sometimes as far south as Keokuk, near the Iowa-Missouri line.

The low dams, built solely for navigation, can provide no control over a flooding upper Mississippi. Witnesses to the big floods of 1965 and 1969 saw as much as 15 feet of water raging through riverfront buildings, and they can expect floods of varying severity about three times a decade. The destructiveness of the 1965 flood brought together representatives of upper river states and the Federal Government to work out the complex solutions to the problem. Meanwhile, some communities have built their levees higher, and some have simply moved back from the river.

At Lock and Dam Number 2, near Hastings, Minnesota, the lockmaster drained some three and a half million gallons of water from the lock basin we waited in, just to drop our small craft to the downstream level. Soon we were watching the clear waters of the St. Croix River mingle with the tan Mississippi. Then we glided down a marked channel past a multitude of islands covered with a tangled growth of trees and thick underbrush. Sandstone cliffs and rolling green hills flanked both sides of the valley.

A few miles downstream, past Lock and Dam Number 3, the river widened into Lake Pepin. Backed up behind a gravel dam built over thousands of years by the inflowing Chippewa River, Pepin forms by far the largest lake between the Twin Cities and the Gulf. Some 22 miles long and as much as 3 miles wide, Lake Pepin affords enough sweep for the wind to pile up spanking whitecaps and occasional storms of dangerous ferocity.

Lakefront towns enjoy a lively business based on water sports. In winter, hundreds of people sit in small heated huts and fish through the ice. In summer, rented houseboats carry families on daylong picnics around the lake. Boats towing water-skiers zigzag across the wakes of lumbering houseboats in dazzling shows of virtuosity. As well they should, for the sport had its start on Lake Pepin at Lake City.

There I met the world's first water-skier, Ralph W. Samuelson, a powerfully built man of 67. When we shook hands, I could easily believe from his grip that he had been able in 1922 to ride on the world's first water skis despite their enormous drag and the slow speed of the boat.

"I got the idea of skiing on water because I missed snow-skiing in summer," he said. "So naturally I tried snow skis first. But boats in those days just didn't have the speed for such skinny boards, so I made this pair."

He pulled from the back of his station wagon two half-inch-thick pine boards eight feet long and nine inches wide with patches of rubber matting and simple leather straps for the feet. They weighed 15 pounds, and I could only guess at the strength required to hang on to the towrope against the drag of those grotesque boards.

"Following a motorboat never bothered me," Ralph said, "but I switched to a 220-horsepower seaplane that took off and, flying four or five feet above the water, towed me at 80 miles an hour. That took a bit of clutching to stay with it. During one exhibition I locked on to that towrope so hard that when I lost the skis I slid for a city block on my stomach before I thought to turn loose."

Ralph put on skiing exhibitions at Palm Beach, Florida, during the 1920's and '30's, and members of the between-wars international set carried the sport with them to the Riviera and from there around the world.

THE FOLLOWING SUNDAY in a drizzly morning mist I rode south from St. Paul on the Burlington Northern, one of the few good passenger railroads remaining in the United States. Pampered by Pullman attendants, I relaxed in the glass observation dome and watched waterfowl dart over the aquatic plants of the magnificent wetlands that stretch along the riverbanks. Rain clouds swirled around bluffs rising steeply from the reedy marshlands. Through holes in the mist loomed the ghosts of islands. The far shore, three miles away in places, was hidden by drifting fog. Enchanted by hints of teeming wildlife in that landscape, soft-edged as a Japanese watercolor, I promised myself a visit to the Upper Mississippi River Wildlife and Fish Refuge, which extends 284 miles along both banks below the bluffs from Lake Pepin to Rock Island, and includes hundreds of river islands.

Next morning at Winona, Minnesota, refuge manager Donald Gray took me on his usual post-weekend boat patrol of the upper reaches of the refuge. With us came assistant manager Bart Foster, a lanky wildlife technician weathered by years of outdoor living. Bart has become known as the tiger of the antilitter patrol, and he was scouring riverbanks and island sandbars for signs of picnic leavings.

"Let's check Mosquito Island—that's a small sandspit about six miles downriver," he said. "Even in yesterday's drippy weather, I counted 200 people picnicking, water-skiing, and swimming there, and that's where we'll find the trash if there's going to be any."

I was astonished to find only a single paper plate, but bit off my congratulations when I discovered that Bart was annoyed that one miscreant had escaped his scrutiny. For Bart has a 60-power zoom glass he sets up on

600-foot-high bluff-top overlooks so he can watch for miles up and down the river, relaying information by radio to a patrol boat. When a careless picnicker is caught and issued a summons, he has no way of knowing Bart's stern eye noted every can or bottle he threw into the bushes. And many good citizens will find out in these lines for the first time why they received a Hound's Tooth Award by postcard. Bart had observed their tidiness and learned their addresses through boat registration numbers.

We continued downstream, and 28 miles and two lockings later Bart swung the boat into a labyrinth of small channels at the delta of Minnesota's Root River. Birches, maples, and elms closed off the sky. Only a ghostly green light filtered through the leafy canopy. A great blue heron flapped across our bow. Striped bass streaked through the water in savage lunges at fingerlings. As we rounded a bend on the Root, nine wood ducks exploded from a raft of green duckweed. Bart nudged the bow against the shore, and we stepped into forest as dim as a cathedral. Overhead, half-grown egrets and great blue herons in the 550 nests of an 80-acre rookery flopped and clattered. Cadavers of half-grown birds littered the forest floor.

"The mortality of egret and heron nestlings from falling is shocking," Don said, "but this rookery, largest of about a dozen in the refuge, has helped bring the egret from near extinction to a healthy, growing population."

Just as important to wildlife as these rookeries, though, are the marshes where ducks and coots—often called mudhens—rest and feed while going to and from their nesting grounds farther north.

Leaving the boat at the refuge headquarters in Winona, we drove north about 30 miles on Wisconsin Highway 35 along the Mississippi, sometimes at water level, sometimes on ledges 200 feet high along the bluffs. At the edge of the Nelson-Trevino Sanctuary we met Jerry Leinecke, district refuge manager, and his student assistant, Steve Thrune, a biology major at Winona State College. We filed in silence to a blind made of reeds at a wooded bend in a slough off the river. Jerry motioned us down and peeked around the blind. Then he pushed the plunger of a detonator box, firing three rockets that looped a net over a flock of wood ducks that had been baited onto a sandbar. He and Steve crashed through the brush to the net and closed it to keep the birds from squirming out. Quickly transferred to burlap bags, the 25 captive birds were banded for studies concerning distribution, annual harvest, and mortality before being released. The whole operation took only half an hour.

"About 10,000 wood ducks are hatched and reared every year on the refuge," Don said, "making it by far the biggest rearing area for wood ducks anywhere on the continent."

Don pointed out signs of the tremendous change in the upper valley's ecology brought about by the 13 locks and dams in the refuge area. "Water levels in the Mississippi used to fluctuate so widely in this valley that its bottomlands couldn't decide what to become—prairie, forest, meadow, or marsh. But the slack-water pools that formed behind the dams in the 1930's eventually resulted in beautiful marshes where hundreds of thousands of birds rest and feed during their spring and fall migrations."

In La Crosse, Wisconsin, I learned that the tranquillity of the river country had lured more than migrating birds. Medical researchers and specialists fleeing large cities have come to the Wisconsin riverbanks.

At the Gundersen Clinic in La Crosse, Dr. E. L. Overholt, head of postgraduate medical education, told me that for years the Midwest had lost doctors to big cities where they could study specialties.

"But now medical centers like ours are luring the young men back, for besides the professional training a big clinic can offer, we give them a beautiful countryside just five minutes from the office."

I chose at random among the specialties and was introduced to Dr. Norman Shealy, a startlingly young neurosurgeon. He had just developed an electronic painkilling tool making it possible for the patient himself to dial as much electric stimulation as needed to inhibit pain.

Dr. Shealy has a particular love for the beauty of the riverbanks. "We think La Crosse is the best spot of all," he said. "Here the bluffs rise sharply 600 or 700 feet above the river—magnificent! We can stand atop them and view the river for 30 miles each way." And Dr. Shealy has put down deep roots during his five years here. He took me on a tour of his Brindabella Farms northeast of La Crosse, where he raises Appaloosas. "Horses thrive in this countryside," he said. "Even at 40 below zero they stay outdoors where they flourish and parasitic worms die."

The leopard-spotted horses crowded about us, scuffling for the best positions to be petted and scratched. Others of his herd of 125 came streaming down the hillside pastures, manes flying and hoofs pounding the lime-rich turf. I well understood the pull of those Wisconsin hills for a young doctor wanting to get away from commuter trains.

*D*ownstream from La Crosse, I traveled before dawn to enjoy the hush along the banks before the sun rising above the bluffs turned the stream a dappled pink and stirred up the bustling world of birds and people. But I was rarely first on the scene, for rising mists revealed boats in midriver with fishermen tending nets. Curious about the health of their fishery, I stopped at Guttenberg, Iowa, to see for myself.

Kenneth E. Saeugling, a commercial fisherman who runs the City Fish Market, took me out for a sunrise tour of his traps. We crossed to an island opposite downtown Guttenberg. There Kenneth rattled off a running conversation as he hauled in nets crammed with carp and buffalo, plus an occasional crappie or northern pike that he threw overboard because sports fish cannot be taken in a commercial haul.

"Don't listen when the crybabies say there're not as many fish as ever," Kenneth said. "Right now is the worst season, and still I took a hundred pounds or more with just a few minutes' work."

He thrashed his nets violently against the side of his boat before slipping them back underwater. "Moss and water plants are getting mighty bad, though. Ruining my nets. Don't know what's making the water plants grow like they've never done before."

Those "mosses," actually algae, made me remember the concern of Dr. Alan J. Brook, head of the department of ecology and behavioral biology at the University of Minnesota. He had felt that overfertilization of river waters by inadequately treated sewage and the runoff from farms and cattle feedlots is slowly but relentlessly choking the river with excessive plant growth. This can have drastic effects on the river's ecology and may threaten the livelihood of Kenneth and 8,500 other full-time and part-time commercial fishermen who in 1968 brought in 53 million pounds of fish.

South from Guttenberg the highway crosses farmlands bursting with prodigious stands of soybeans and corn, but the landscape had been ravaged by Dutch elm disease. The skeletons of tens of thousands of once stately trees stood stark and desolate against the sky. When I breakfasted in Dubuque I read in the paper an advertisement for bids on cutting 150 dead trees that had once formed the famed "Cathedral Arch" down Rhomberg Avenue to the river. In all, Dubuque had lost 6,000 trees.

On the waterfront at the Dubuque Boat and Boiler Company shipyard, Henry B. Miller showed me through a steam stern-wheeler his company was building as a 400-passenger sightseeing and party excursion boat for the Illinois River at Peoria.

"So far as we know this *Julia Belle Swain* will be the last paddle-wheel steamboat ever built. Too bad, because people love steam. They like the slow majestic thrust of the pistons, the hissing steam. Beats that nervous little poppety-popping of diesels all hollow.

"But the pinch comes in finding engines. They were all built to order in the old days, and they were cut up with the boat when it went out of service. When we heard the Baton Rouge ferry company was going out of business, we raced down to Louisiana and bought the engines on the *City of Baton Rouge*. They were built in 1906, but I wish my six-month-old car ran as well. I have no idea where to find another engine, though, if someday another customer wants a steamboat built."

So the once-booming business of building river steamboats may indeed come to a close exactly 160 years after the *New Orleans* slid down the ways at Pittsburgh and opened the glamorous era of puffing river packets.

Weekend homes, snug boathouses crowd the riverbank at La Crosse, Wisconsin. Though these craft never leave their moorings, mobile houseboats by the hundred cruise the tree-lined upper reaches of the Mississippi during the summer months.

48

Falls of St. Anthony in 1848 plunges among river islands marking the future site of the Twin Cities. Today, tamed by erosion and engineering, the cascade lies dammed between two bridges at Minneapolis (below); shipping moves through a lock along the far bank. Giant grain elevators and skyscrapers now rise where an early explorer once viewed "gentle ascents, which in the summer are covered with the finest verdure and interspersed with little groves, that give a pleasing variety to the prospect."

Summer's delights: Young-
sters take a cooling swing
into the river at Champlin,
Minnesota, and wait for fish
to bite near Monticello. At
sunset a water-skier zigzags
across Lake Pepin, where the
sport originated in 1922.
Student guides in infantry
field uniforms of the 1820's
fire a volley of blanks during
musket drill at the Fort
Snelling Restoration, just
south of Minneapolis.

Clamming rigs yield their harvest to the Lessard family (above) at Prairie du Chien, Wisconsin. The mollusks reflexively close when touched by the drag hooks. Below, carp fill a seine on Lake Pepin. Water-splashed Ralph Richtman of Trempealeau (opposite), a third-generation river pilot and fisherman, has worked on the Mississippi 40 years; his grandchildren "would live on the river, swim, fish, or help me catch minnows all summer if they could."

Flash floods of May 1970 leave devastation in southeastern Minnesota. Torrents dragged the car a mile off the road and swept the driver's body another four miles. At Lake City, David Plank watches brother Wayne scrape mud from a bicycle. Relatives console Dixie Rabehl at her Millville farm, ravaged by nearby Spring Creek.

Horse-drawn omnibus carries tourists 75 years into the past at Stone-
field, a pioneer village re-created near Cassville, Wisconsin. A carpen-
ter shop, general store, and other emporiums surround the square
below. In the Photograph Studio visitors pose before a river backdrop.

Life on the Mississippi means hard work for Iowa crane operator Jack Hitchcock, who lifts steel plates into position for the Dubuque Boat and Boiler Company; since 1927 he has helped build river craft and ocean-going ships; 19-year-old David Bender, drill in

hand, shapes and welds hull plates. Gretchen Vera (opposite, left) and Lesley Ann Lagen cool off at Nine Mile Island, a beach near Dubuque. On a warm Sunday afternoon in Eagle Point Park, John Liebold hands out barbecue assignments to picnicking children.

"The Town That Time Forgot," Galena, Illinois, inspires local artist Barney Moore (below). In the 1850's nearby lead mines played out, and a slow decline began. Few new structures replaced fine old ones built by mining fortunes. Lifetime resident Vic T. Kohlbauer (opposite lower) recalls the renaissance that began in Galena about 1960 when people from St. Louis and Chicago discovered its 19th-century charm and quiet. Artist Jo Mead (opposite upper) renovated a brewery for a year-round home.

Spring comes to the upper Mississippi as the first towboat of the year pushes a barge fleet upstream through breaking ice above Cassville. Since World War II, barge traffic the length of the river has increased steadily; diesel-powered towboats move ten times more tonnage annually than steamboats did in their heyday. New high-capacity barges carry 85,000 bushels of grain or more than a million gallons of oil. Lashed together with steel cables, a fleet may measure more than 1,000 feet, longer than many ocean liners.

Patchwork of cars blankets the riverside yard of the Burlington Northern at Hannibal, Missouri. Spreading

Wine, Cheese, and Honey

the 1850's, railroads encouraged the rapid development of the rich western Mississippi basin.

A HUNDRED MILES OR SO below Dubuque as the river winds, or 70 miles via U. S. 61 if you're in a hurry, the Quad Cities — all five of them — spread from either bank of the Mississippi. The 500 major industrial firms of Rock Island, Moline, and East Moline, Illinois, together with Davenport, Iowa, and its late-sprouting next-door neighbor Bettendorf, directly or indirectly provide the 370,000 citizens of the area with a buying income of well over a billion dollars a year. In Moline alone, where in 1847 John Deere began producing the first self-polishing steel plow, 84 manufacturers turn out more than two and a half billion dollars' worth of industrial products, including machine tools, truck bodies, freight and passenger elevators, ball bearings, and, of course, farm equipment. The pioneer plowmaker whose dream it was to improve the life of tillers of Corn Belt soil would be amazed to see the fantastic array of planters, combines, harrows, and plows that rolls off the production lines of Deere & Company's Moline factory today. International Harvester, Caterpillar Tractor, and J. I. Case also have plants in the Quad Cities, giving the metropolis a firm hold on the title of "Farm Machinery Capital of the World."

Moline mushroomed into the industrial nucleus of the Quad Cities after it was connected by rail in 1856 with Davenport and farmlands west of the Mississippi. Because I had seen factory towns before with their soot-spewing chimneys and urban decay, I approached the juncture of the Mississippi and Rock Rivers with foreboding.

Following telephoned instructions of Deere & Company's Rey Brune on how to find the headquarters building, I drove through Moline southeastward beyond the farthest suburbs. Puzzled, I searched the farmland on either side for buildings with sawtooth roofs and smoking stacks. Instead, I found a rolling park with twin lakes and hundreds of spraying fountains. Beyond the lakes stood the firm's Administrative Center, a building of cinnamon-colored steel and bronze-tinted glass — powerful, squat, and yet oddly graceful like a karate champion.

Rey told me the architect was Eero Saarinen — a man virtually deified in his Finnish homeland where architects command the respect we reserve for professional quarterbacks. Of the coarse-textured structure, my host explained: "The high-tensile steel used by Saarinen in this building never requires painting. Left to weather, it forms a striking rust patina that protects it from deterioration."

Corridors and offices display paintings by Grant Wood, Japanese sculptures, Brazilian oils, Yugoslav tapestries, Spanish wood carvings, and other works of art from some of the countries where Deere & Company has factories and sales outlets.

"Few of us can afford to collect art as fine as this," Rey said, "yet here we spend many of our waking hours surrounded by it."

Reluctant to confess that I just might have grievously misjudged the Quad Cities, I slyly asked if I could visit a real production center — a smoky foundry, for instance. Rey took me to the Deere Foundry opened in East Moline in 1969, a showcase for Quad Cities industry.

Any foundry I've ever visited has been a stygian cavern lit by tongues of flame reflected from rolling plumes of smoke — a backdrop for a scene from Dante's *Inferno*. Rey showed me a foundry that annually turns out 80,000 tons of 2-pound to 600-pound castings for tractors and other machinery — but without a single stack to ventilate the 15 acres that lie under one roof.

Inside, electric arc furnaces spewed fumes; ladles carrying molten iron to holding furnaces glowed white hot; cores cooked in ovens; all foundry operations that give off blackening smoke progressed apace.

But the air stayed clear, for a collecting system sucked up the dust-laden smoke, passed it through scrubbers, and returned the air to the outdoors cleaner than it had come in. Indeed, the air pumped into the building had been scrubbed first, so that foundrymen pass their workdays in an environment cleaner than that of their own backyards. The dirt filtered out is squeezed into pellets and carried to another end of the 315-acre tract to fill a swamp for future expansion of the foundry.

Factory chimneys still exist in the Quad Cities, of course. But Deere & Company began pioneering new methods of air-pollution control as early as the 1920's, long before policing the atmosphere began in earnest nationally. And since the mid-1950's the firm has taken a leading role in community projects to counter water pollution as well.

In fact, the whole community of the Quad Cities shows an interest in a comfortable environment. Suburban settlements have small-city charm and convenience. The riverside is sprinkled with tree-shaded parks as well as marinas and commercial docks. Museums display early farm implements along with stone tools of the Sauk and Fox Indians. Theaters bring in road companies offering Broadway hits.

Crossing the river to Davenport, I remembered one of Abraham Lincoln's lesser-known gifts to American posterity. In 1856 the first railroad bridge across the Mississippi took advantage of Rock Island's stepping-stone position in midstream to avoid an awkwardly long single overwater span. Steamboaters raged against the threat of competition and what they called obstruction of river channels by bridge piers.

In May 1856, a scant two weeks after the first locomotive crossing, the steamboat *Effie Afton* hit one of the piers and burned. The boat owners brought suit for a showdown on whether to allow bridges across the river. The railroad hired three lawyers, among them Abraham Lincoln, just five years from the Presidency. He presented his case in favor of river bridges with an argument that would become known as the Lincoln Doctrine by the time the issue was finally settled in the Supreme Court in 1862. As interpreted by lawyers in a suit in 1858, the doctrine reads:

"... A man has as good right to go across a river as another has to go up or down the river ... the existence of a bridge which does not prevent or unreasonably obstruct navigation is not inconsistent with the navigable character of the stream."

The Rock Island bridge no longer threatens the "navigable character" of the Mississippi, for towboats and barges now travel that stretch under the bridge through locks as wide as those of the Panama Canal.

In 1970 more than 2,800 commercial towboats used the locks, pushing some 14,500 barges loaded with 16 million tons of commodities. Of this, 10 million tons were loaded or unloaded at the Rock Island docks. Barges bound upstream carry petroleum, coal, salt, molasses, asphalt, ammonia, and steel. The main product moving downstream from the Quad Cities is grain, much of it taken aboard on the Iowa side.

For more than five decades, Muscatine, Iowa, 25 miles south of Davenport, drew a large part of its livelihood from the Mississippi, making buttons from mother-of-pearl blanks cut out of clamshells. When plastic imitations came on the market after World War II, Muscatine manufacturers adopted the new material, and the city remained one of the largest button-making centers in the United States. Of the three button factories still in business in the city, all have converted to plastic, the last in 1967. But they maintain large inventories of pearl buttons, looking hopefully to a day when the more expensive fasteners again will be in demand.

Richard Massey, who in 1969 bought the stock of a company going out of business, sees another market. He took me through a warehouse holding 144 million pearl buttons in 4,000 combinations of size, shape, color, and pattern, all catalogued and stored by the gross in boxes.

"Muscatine alone used to make several times this many mother-of-pearl buttons a year," Richard said. "Now nobody in the world makes a single one. So these will grow in value as collectors learn about them."

He showed me ringed fisheyes, metal shanks, French cuts, buckles for dress belts and shoes—a hundred variations on mother-of-pearl fastenings. "I started selling a month ago," he said. "A part-time preacher carries samples to county fairs and centennial celebrations. He sets up a booth and sells like mad."

Fishermen continue to work the Mississippi River clambeds to supply Japan with bits of shell for use as seeds for cultured pearls. Searching the free world for shells to replace the ones previously obtained from China's Yangtze River, the Japanese found those in the Mississippi and some of its tributaries to have the right degree of hardness. They cut the shells into dice, tumble them in sand and pumice until they round to spheres, and tuck them into healthy oysters, which in turn coat the clamshell irritants with layers of softly glowing nacre to form pearls.

I drove south on the Iowa side, through Burlington — perched atop steep bluffs that gave the onetime lumbering center its original name, Flint Hills — and on downward toward low-lying Fort Madison, maker of ball-point pens, ink, fertilizer, chemicals, paper products, and tools and dies.

On the riverbank below Burlington I ran across Gayle Heater, a stocky composing-room man on the local newspaper who also works as a commercial fisherman. When I told him of the optimistic assessment of river fisheries I had heard at Guttenberg, Gayle exploded.

"Look at that pile of mud and smartweed you're standing on. Three weeks ago where you're standing dryshod, you'd have been hock-deep in water. And it'll be another three weeks before the dams can adjust the water level again. No fish can flop around for very long on dry land. Mud just ain't no right home for a fish."

Bill Conrad, an 81-year-old fisherman, joined in. "I put out a trotline for a week and caught one carp and two little catfish." His eyes twinkled. "Course I didn't have time to poach your traps, Gayle, or I might of done better."

Gayle looked over the river with disgust.

"Once you could drink out of midchannel. Now a hog wouldn't wash his feet in it. See where Conrad's net buoy shows out there? I used to sink my fish baskets 30 feet deep on that spot. Now the kids wade there for kicks."

We rode a few blocks in Gayle's car to the Buffalo Tap, a riverside gathering place for fishermen. There Gayle argued that Government dams slow down currents and let suspended silt deposit along the shores.

"The Engineers don't care nothing about fishermen," he said. "Only them towboats. Pretty soon they going to have only a navigation channel here running between banks of dredger spoil, and then they'll be happy. I'd like to see a plague take them dams."

A roar of dissent came from the other end of the bar. "Before the dams, we had low-water times when the river almost disappeared," another fisherman retorted. "The dams keep some water in the lakes all the time."

"The steamboats did all right and the fish did a lot better before the dams," Gayle insisted. "Why, back fifty years ago there were so many fish in the river that Catfish Kelly kept his gar Old Rhodes tied up to the Fort Madison bridge. He had one red eye and one green eye and he'd blink them like a traffic light to control the fish traffic up and down stream. Now he's buried in the mud and gone."

My mind flashed back to a Minnesota lakeside cabin porch where I had listened weeks earlier to vireos, flycatchers, and loons saluting the setting sun. With me was Dr. Samuel Eddy, fish curator emeritus at the University of Minnesota. Dr. Eddy reminisced about the good old days of fishing the Mississippi in his youth.

"The Falls of St. Anthony used to cut the river into two ecosystems," Dr. Eddy said. "Migrating species from the south could never climb the waterfall. But when the first dam went in at Keokuk in 1913, disruption of fish traffic began to occur there, some 500 miles downstream. The dam also destroyed important commercial clambeds of a species that spent part of its larval stage as a parasite on the river herring, a great migrator. Where the herring went the clam went, but no farther." Both species soon disappeared from the river above the dam because the herring could not swim through the turbulent waters of the spillways.

Other species of clams, however, travel with nonmigrating fish while in the larval stage, and in recent years fishermen have found large new clambeds with good quality shells north of Keokuk.

The Corps of Engineers itself acknowledges that the dams flooded certain favorite fishing spots of old-timers but maintains that higher water levels behind the dams have provided better fishing conditions than ever during times of low flow.

When I slipped out of the Buffalo Tap, the debate was still raging over the worth of the Government lock and dam system.

A T NAUVOO, Illinois, 25 miles downstream from Burlington, I found youthful Brigham Young University students working at improbable tasks. These young men crouched in a vacant lot, digging with small shovels and trowels under the eye of a stern-looking elder. Introducing himself, J. Byron Ravsten, resident manager of the Mormons' Nauvoo restoration project, explained that the students were using sound archeological methods to dig up evidence of Mormon greatness in 19th-century Illinois.

On this site once prospered a community of 15,000—in its day second only to Chicago as Illinois' most populous city—founded by Mormon leader Joseph Smith in 1839. Members of his Church of Jesus Christ of Latter-day Saints, practicing the belief that all nonmembers must be saved from paganism, were forced by bitter hostility to flee first from Ohio and then from Missouri. From there Smith and his followers trekked northeastward, crossed the Mississippi, and settled along a quiet bend in the river. Nauvoo, "beautiful place," Smith called it, using a name he derived from Hebrew. But Nauvoo brought no respite from religious persecution. In June 1844 Smith was imprisoned and soon was shot to death by a mob that broke into the jail. Six months later the state, having repealed the city's charter, ordered its residents to leave. Finally, in 1846, the Mormons abandoned their colony, and five thousand of them joined Brigham Young in what was to become the largest single migration in the history of the United States, 1,500 miles overland to the "promised land" of Utah.

"This westward migration from Nauvoo consisted of a city on wheels," Byron explained. "There were blacksmiths, printers, tailors, bakers, wainwrights, coopers, stonemasons—all the artisans that were needed to build an instant and thriving metropolis after the Mormons arrived at Salt Lake. When the forty-niners on the great trek west reached Salt Lake City just a year or so later, they found a flourishing base to replenish their stocks and repair their worn equipment.

"It all started here at Nauvoo, and we want to restore the old town to tell the American people the story."

Byron took me by his headquarters, a handsome cut-stone structure built of materials salvaged from the Nauvoo Mormon Temple after it was gutted by an arsonist in 1848 and further damaged by a tornado two years later. The building once had served as the dining hall for a communistic community of Frenchmen called Icarians. They had occupied Nauvoo after learning that the Mormons had abandoned it. I winced when I heard that the fine old structure might be demolished to make room for a headquarters building compatible with the older Mormon architecture, but I brightened at the mention of the French Icarians. Byron directed me to a descendant, Miss Lillian M. Snyder, also an amateur historian.

Miss Snyder knew the story of the Icarians well. She was preparing a paper on the subject for a gathering of the descendants.

"In early 19th-century France," she told me, "Étienne Cabet agitated for socialist reforms so successfully that in 1835 King Louis Philippe exiled him for five years. In England, he planned a utopian socialist democracy called Icaria. So nearly perfect did it seem that hundreds of thousands of Frenchmen eventually became converts.

"Gathering a small band of disciples, he sailed for the New World to found his Icaria in 1849 at Nauvoo, where his followers bought some of the town's empty buildings from the Mormons and rented their fields.

"But the colony existed only a few years. By the fall of 1860 the remnants of utopia at Nauvoo had shattered against the realities of internal political strife and crop failure. Most of the colonists sold their property and scattered from the ill-fated city."

A few stayed, however — among them ancestors of Fred J. Baxter, who continues the Gallic business of winemaking as part owner of Gem City Vineland Company, the only vintners in Illinois who grow their own grapes.

"My great-grandfather acted as secretary to the Icarians," Fred told me. "He stayed on after the big split and, like a good Frenchman, started a vineyard. Now we grow a million pounds of grapes and press about one-third of them to make 50,000 bottles of sauterne and Concord red wine. A few more grapes make fresh juice and the rest grace midwestern tables as dessert in season. We'll probably never know if our wine travels well, for it is all consumed before it gets much more than a hundred miles away."

In the winery, Fred showed me an assortment of great casks ranging from 70-gallon brandy barrels stamped with faded Spanish legends to modern 3,000-gallon containers.

"This oval-shaped 540-gallon cask arrived at Nauvoo in 1852 and we still use it. Some say it held water, but if I know my French ancestors it never held anything but wine."

As we talked, Fred called my attention to another Nauvoo industry with

European overtones. At Nauvoo Milk Products Company, Bill Scully, the president, took me through the plant, built at the site of an old brewery on the bank of the Mississippi. There he makes blue cheese with milk trucked from dairies 200 miles around in Illinois and Iowa.

After the milk coagulates, the curd is drained and powdered with *Penicillium roqueforti,* the mold that makes the green veins and imparts flavor to blue cheese. Then cheesemakers hand-rub salt into the wheels, perforate them with needles to let air in for best mold growth, and stack them for curing in caves that once stored beer.

"Blue cheese comes from six other American factories," Bill said, "but our plant is the only one in Illinois. It was established here because of Prohibition, which made several arched stone cellars obsolete for beer manufacture—just at the time Iowa State University proved that a fine blue cheese could be made in the United States if that kind of curing cellar became available."

*B*EFORE DRIVING SOUTH along the riverbank, I put a wheel of blue cheese into the car with the bottles of Nauvoo wine and an aromatic loaf of dark-brown bread from a Nauvoo baker who mills his own flour to be sure he gets the whole grain. For simple beauty the 12-mile drive to Hamilton rivaled a spin beside a Scottish loch. A line of trees on the narrow shoulder between highway and river provided a frame for magnificent vistas of the stream and of Iowa parkland.

At Hamilton, just before crossing to Keokuk, I spotted an old brick factory marked "Dadant and Sons, Beekeepers' Supplies." The French name prompted me to drop in to see if I had found an Icarian offshoot.

But Charles (Chuck) Dadant, one of the present operators, said greatgrandfather Charles came to Illinois independently in 1863 from the Champagne region of France. Naturally, he first tried his hand at making wine. He soon found that his vines made poor wine but provided nectar for splendid honey. A minister in Pennsylvania had just invented the slide-tray hive; Dadant adopted and improved it, and wrote so prolifically and enthusiastically to beekeepers in European countries that he drove the old-fashioned conical straw hive off the market. So the familiar square wooden beehive found all over the world today traces back to a modest brick factory in an Illinois hamlet.

But bigger things were happening there than hive design.

Chuck took me to a small hybridizing laboratory to meet Dr. G. H. (Bud) Cale, Jr. Chuck assured me that Bud ranks among the half-dozen bee geneticists in the world and probably is the best of that rare company.

Bud has hybridized bees to develop colonies with specific qualities— gentleness, for instance. He demonstrated this to me by scooping up a handful of buzzing bees and spreading them on his arm without injury.

"Until recently we bred bees to produce honey and wax. But the Maker did not intend that to be the bee's only function. He meant them to pollinate plants. A lot of other insects helped, of course, but in vast areas of the world today, farmers have become so efficient at wiping out insect pests that they have also wiped out the native pollinating insect population."

So the big business for the modern beekeeper lies in renting his colonies to orchardists, truck farmers, and seed growers to ensure fruitful crops where native insects have been exterminated.

"Bees have finicky tastes, and this creates problems," Bud said. "If we set out ordinary colonies in a California alfalfa seed field, they'll sneak off to work what the seed man might call weeds because all flowers compete for the bee's attention. Melons, star thistles, morning glories—anything that blooms—lure bees off the alfalfa job. A safflower plant carries something resembling a hundred dandelion flowers on each stalk, making it a tremendously attractive competitor. But we've managed—by selection and inbreeding of colonies showing a slightly more than normal taste for alfalfa —to produce colonies that prefer it to other plants.

"California has 200,000 acres of seed alfalfa and few surviving pollinating insects in the alfalfa-growing regions. Without bees, an acre produces 100 pounds of seed, with bees 500 pounds, with our alfalfa-specific hybrids we hope for 800 to 1,000 pounds."

Since the native insects' function has been replaced by Bud's hybrids, probably nobody mourns the passing of trillions of California's lowly pollinators—except for the songbirds, of course, which may vanish too, and thus bring about the dreaded silent spring.

That evening at my Keokuk motel I unloaded my car and snacked on dark-brown, wheaty-tasting Nauvoo bread spread with Nauvoo blue cheese and Hamilton honey, enhanced by Nauvoo wine.

Next day, driving 50 miles south to Hannibal, Missouri, I discovered that a drought which had worsened a plague of southern corn wilt had broken with a violent thunderstorm. Twisted sheets of galvanized roofing littered the road. The fury of midwestern prairie winds showed clearly in tree limbs strewn about the fields, but farmers lounging at gas stations cheerily accepted the damage in exchange for the life-giving rain.

Hannibal once had 54 passenger trains daily—none stops there now— and operated sawmills that converted logs from Wisconsin and Minnesota forests to the lumber that built the Midwest. Wandering in Hannibal today, you would soon realize that some things haven't changed much since 1853 when a lad of 18 named Samuel Clemens left town to become a literary giant. Signs advertise hotels, restaurants, museums, tearooms, and shopping centers with names taken from virtually every major character in Mark Twain's tales about Tom Sawyer and Huckleberry Finn.

"There is even one place named for Injun Joe, unquestionably one of the most scurrilous characters in American fiction," said Charles Rendlen, Jr., an attorney who serves on a committee that seeks to redirect the town's exploitation of its favorite son.

"But fortunately time hasn't destroyed the historic area entirely. The section has expanded very little, and cobblestones downtown still lie under the asphalt and a wooden road under that.

"In three years, we have reversed Hannibal's decay in the old town. We have an ice-cream parlor, a tintype photographer, antique shops, a summer-stock theater, and other tourist services in authentic period buildings. Now we must raise money to buy out downtown owners who don't want to remodel according to our architect's plan for rebuilding Hannibal as it looked in Twain's day."

Walking through the historic area—tentatively called St. Petersburg after Tom Sawyer's fictitious hometown—Rendlen showed me sites for restaurants, clothing stores, printing plants (young Clemens worked as a printer's devil in his brother's printshop), and other businesses compatible with a historic quarter. And he pointed out that on 200-foot-high bluffs above the river the town has well-preserved residential areas that predate the Civil War.

Today, Hannibal is a small industrial center serving communities on the surrounding plains of Illinois and Missouri. Heavy barges glide by, a few stopping to load grain or to unload logs and ammonia. With a population of less than 20,000, the city employs more than 2,000 workers in 26 industries. It produces shoes, cigars, cement, steel, lumber, and metal products— carried to market overnight by train and truck.

Looking back on his Hannibal boyhood in *Life on the Mississippi*, Twain remembered grand vistas of "the magnificent Mississippi, rolling its mile-wide tide along, shining in the sun." That rolling tide soon lured him to St. Louis, then a bustling city of 80,000.

Only from the air can today's traveler fully understand the tremendous power of the site of St. Louis, which Twain saw as "a great and prosperous and advancing city...." From the west the Missouri snakes in, a mud-laden watercourse that rises 2,533 miles upstream in far-off Montana and brings together the waters of tributaries that drain the northeastern slopes of the Rockies and the northern Great Plains. From the east comes the Illinois River bearing the commerce of Chicago and the industrial cities of the Illinois hinterland, giving access to the Great Lakes and ultimately to the Atlantic Ocean via the St. Lawrence Seaway.

Just beyond the juncture of the rivers gleams the great St. Louis arch, "Gateway to the West."

Spinning and bowing, a "fancy dancer" matches intricate footwork to the beat of drums. He performs in the Labor Day Indian Pow-Wow at Black Hawk State Park, Rock Island, Illinois, where the Sauk and Fox tribes share their ceremonial heritage.

In the solitude of his weed-choked boatyard at Rock Island, Illinois, Fred Kahlke takes his ease in the glow of afternoon. During the golden days of steamboating, Kahlke Bros. Ship Yards launched scores of proud stern-wheelers. The W. J. Quinlan *(left)*, built there in 1904, served most of her 41 years as a nickel ferry between Rock Island and Davenport, Iowa. Today, pleasure craft like the outboard at right roam the river.

Riverside cornucopia: Her basket overflowing with Concord grapes,
a picker samples the rich harvest of a vineyard at Nauvoo, Illinois.
Across the Mississippi in northern Iowa, farmlands green the country-
side near Balltown; trees edge the distant river. Downstream near
Le Claire, an earthy haze surrounds a farmer during spring planting.

Heading downriver at Keokuk, Iowa, a tow-boat pushes barges out of Lock No. 19, one of the largest on the Mississippi River. Water ponded above the adjoining dam

spins turbines in the power plant of the Union Electric Company at right. Visitors (opposite) view its generator room. A crewman (opposite, lower) rests on a hawser-strewn barge inside the 110-by-1,200-foot lock; to raise or lower vessels 38.2 feet requires about ten minutes. The stern-wheeler excursion boat Addie May (below) awaits passengers.

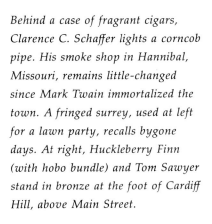

Behind a case of fragrant cigars,
Clarence C. Schaffer lights a corncob
pipe. His smoke shop in Hannibal,
Missouri, remains little-changed
since Mark Twain immortalized the
town. A fringed surrey, used at left
for a lawn party, recalls bygone
days. At right, Huckleberry Finn
(with hobo bundle) and Tom Sawyer
stand in bronze at the foot of Cardiff
Hill, above Main Street.

Mississippi River pilot, printer, author, publisher, and lecturer, Mark Twain returned in his imagination to his boyhood home for the themes of his most memorable books. Hannibal's waterfront (below), sketched by English artist Henry Lewis about 1848, appears as Twain knew it. In the first illustrated edition of The Adventures of Tom Sawyer, published in 1876, the hero (left) persuades a friend to pay for the privilege of whitewashing Aunt Polly's fence.

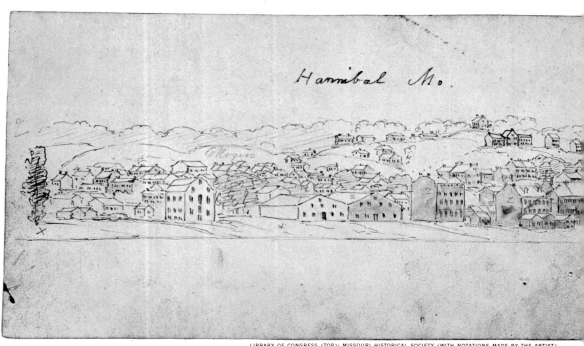

Hannibal Mo.

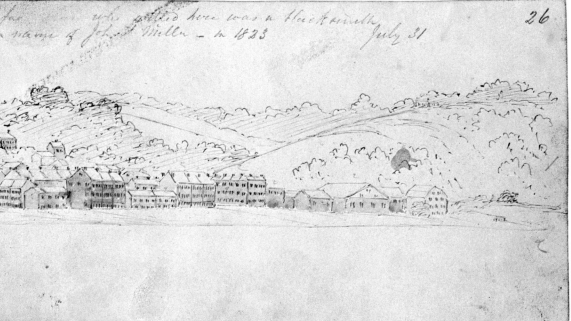

26

Flinging whitewash and caution to the winds, David DeLaPorte of Hannibal wins the 1970 National Fence Painting Contest. Lynn Shores and Brent Beard, as "Becky and Tom," the town's official greeters for 1970, explore Mark Twain Cave, haunt of the infamous Injun Joe.

Steamboats crowd the riverfront at St. Louis, where in 1874 the famed Eads Bridge opened to trains and wag

"Old Man River" Begins

nking rail traffic east and west of the river, the span hastened the end of the steamboat era.

A MIDCONTINENT RIVERFRONT made St. Louis. Founded by Frenchmen in 1764 on the west bank of the Mississippi, the settlement flourished for a hundred years as a transport center and as a trading post for furs brought down the Missouri for boating to New Orleans. Trappers and explorers, Meriwether Lewis and William Clark among them, used the frontier village as an outfitting point for close to half a century.

Beginning in 1803 with America's purchase of the Louisiana Territory, St. Louis became the gateway to the West for pioneers pouring across the Alleghenies and down the Ohio River. They changed the town's language and character — and expanded it far beyond its fortified strip of three streets paralleling less than a mile of riverfront.

The first steamboat came to St. Louis in 1817, and soon craft from the Missouri, the Ohio, and the upper and lower Mississippi moored three and four deep alongside the city's levees. Bigger and faster, the new vessels took over from flatboats and keelboats the job of moving furs and supplies, and later of transporting lead, lumber, grain, and people. In 1860 St. Louis logged in more than 5,000 steamboat arrivals.

Ten years later, on July 4, the steamboat age put on a show of pyrotechnical brilliance just before it guttered out like a spent skyrocket. The *Robert E. Lee* arrived from New Orleans, some 1,200 miles downstream, six and a half hours ahead of the *Natchez* to win the most famous boat race in American history in a run of 90 hours and 14 minutes.

A century later to the day, I stood on the cobblestoned slope of St. Louis's historic waterfront and cheered William Petty of Ohio as he roared upriver in a boat powered by twin 140-horsepower outboards. With a time of 22 hours and 27 minutes, he was winner of a three-boat race from New Orleans, now almost 200 miles closer because cutoffs — all but one of them man-made — have eliminated more than a dozen bends.

The difference in the size of the crowds cheering the victors was a measure of the city's growth away from its original riverfront. A century ago tens of thousands watched Captain John W. Cannon bring his steamboat in first. Scarcely 500 spectators — city officials, history buffs, and visitors waiting to ride to the top of the nearby Gateway Arch — cheered William Petty across the line. But at the three general-cargo docks and at 40 specialized terminals along some 20 miles of St. Louis riverfront and the Illinois bank opposite, thousands of men were at work. Onto scores of steel barges they loaded grain, coal, vegetable oils, gasoline, chemicals, sand, crushed rock; they unloaded steel, cement, minerals, petroleum products.

Railroads struck down the steamboat era, and the Eads Bridge at St. Louis, completed in 1874 and still in service, delivered the *coup de grace*. Railroad bridges, and later highway bridges, switched the main direction of commerce from north-south to east-west. In 1910, poorest year of the era, only 559 steamboat arrivals were recorded at St. Louis. With World War I, however, a pressing need for transport brought a revival of river traffic, and barges pushed by paddle-wheel steamers carried the freight. In the 1930's diesel towboats began nudging out the steam vessels and by the 1950's had replaced them entirely.

Towboats bring far more tonnage to St. Louis than the steamboats ever did, pushing up to 40 steel barges lashed together in a five-acre platform, but they tie up at docks so scattered that many of the 2,500,000 people of metropolitan St. Louis scarcely know a river runs by their door.

In the late 1930's most of the little-used warehouses and other buildings along the historic waterfront were torn down. The city spared the old cathedral and the courthouse where Dred Scott's case for freedom from slavery was first pleaded, and where slaves were auctioned on the steps. Today the Gateway Arch soars 630 feet above a green park bordered on the land side by a row of modern buildings and on the river side by three steamboats, engineless relics of their era. They offer food, Dixieland music, old-time melodrama, and nostalgia.

The jet fighter, rocket, and spacecraft, not the towboat, have replaced the steamboat as the glamour craft of St. Louis. In a metropolis booming with the production of aircraft, automobiles, railway equipment, beer, shoes, and chemicals, McDonnell Douglas Corporation is the Mississippi Valley's largest industrial employer, providing jobs for 32,000 people.

At a sprawling complex northwest of the city, I saw McDonnell men building the F-4, proven repeatedly over a decade to be one of the world's hottest and toughest fighter-bombers. And those workers were getting ready to build an even more maneuverable jet, the F-15.

Elsewhere in the plant workmen swarmed over an open-ended cylinder as big as a house trailer, the air-lock module of the space station Skylab, scheduled for launching in 1973. After the Skylab cluster—air lock, telescope mount, and workshop—is sent into orbit 235 miles high, a space vehicle with a three-man crew will go aloft and dock with it. The astronauts will go through the air lock into the workshop, where they will stay for 28 days of experiments. After their return to earth, two other teams will go up in turn, each for 56 days. A life-support system in the air lock will provide the spacemen with vital needs: air, electrical power, communications, computer data. In addition, the air lock will permit the astronauts to sortie into space in pressurized suits without depressurizing the workshop.

More typical of St. Louis to most people is another gigantic industry, beer-making. The Anheuser-Busch plant, world's biggest brewery, spreads over 70 city blocks and includes 63 buildings—one of them, the Brew House, has been designated a National Historic Landmark. In 1970 the company's scattered breweries turned out more than 22 million barrels of beer, better than a third of them at the vast St. Louis plant.

I toured many of the buildings and stopped on the top floor of the 80-year-old Brew House, still in use, to look down into a central well decorated with Victorian rococo exuberance. Bronze hop vines twine the length of immense chandeliers, and gilt acanthus leaves wreathe the capitals of the interior columns.

Andrew Steinhubl, the St. Louis brewmaster, told me that the plant always has a million barrels filled with beer in various stages—and every afternoon he takes part in a tasting session. Almost three million bottles pass down the line daily, forcing inspectors to change jobs every half hour to keep from becoming hypnotized. And nearly nine million cans also leave the plant every day.

To make a barrel of beer takes up to 15 barrels of water, mostly for washing tanks and for the pasteurizing process, so Andy draws nine million gallons daily from the city system and takes six million more from the river to be filtered in the brewery.

Impressed though I was by the gargantuan flood, I found more fascination in the pilot brewery for flavor research—a complete pygmy plant with a half-barrel daily capacity, just right for home brewing. "It would make a great Christmas gift for a beer drinker," Andy confirmed. "That is, if you have $100,000 to buy one like it."

To many, St. Louis means three things—that big brewery, the name of Lindbergh's airplane, and a zoo world-famous for its performing-animal shows and naturalistic settings for its wildlife. I toured the zoo by golf cart with director William Hoff. At the bear pit I was struck by the similarity of its background to palisades along the Mississippi. "There should be a resemblance," Bill said. "We took plaster casts of the limestone bluffs downstream at Herculaneum and used them as forms for these concrete palisades. Zoos all over the United States have used our casts to make backgrounds for their bear exhibits."

We went inside the tank room where Siegfried, a 3,000-pound walrus, splashed in air-conditioned comfort though the outside temperature hovered around 100° F. On trips through the Arctic, I have seen thousands of walrus and on one desperate occasion lived for days on walrus liver. But I had never before been within 18 inches of a live walrus and I was apprehensive as he crowded me against the closed door, flopping about, grunting, and excitedly stretching his bristly nose toward me.

The keeper warned me, "He tries to show his affection by hugging you, and then taking you to the bottom of the pool." I skipped backward when Siegfried tried to wrap one of his flippers around my knees. Quick as a cat, he flopped the other around the keeper, who escaped Siegfried's dangerous love by slipping out of his boot. Finally, Siegfried took to his pool, wrapped his flippers around a log, and carried it to the bottom.

Fish from the Mississippi swim in the aquatic exhibit of the Children's Zoo, a series of buildings covered with earth so that the area looks like low wooded hills. "We sieve the fish from water pockets—sloughs—left when the river recedes from high water," said Charles H. Hoessle, general curator of the zoo. "And what a fantastic variety we've taken in the past year or two. The usual river fish like carp, drum, shad, channel catfish, buffalo, and some like the sturgeon and spoonbill catfish that haven't been seen in the river around St. Louis for 10, maybe 15 years." He speculated that these pollution-sensitive fish are reappearing because the waters of the exceptionally wet years just past have diluted the poisons. "Farmers along the river harvest the stranded fish too," he added. "They used to have big fish fries to use them up, but nowadays they freeze some, put some in their farm ponds, and return the rest to the river."

ECAUSE of large Indian earthworks in the vicinity, St. Louis in its early days was known as "Mound City." Many had to be torn down before the town could expand. Some of the mounds, built by a people who had created the Mississippian culture by A.D. 850, still stand scattered about the area. Perhaps by colonization, the culture spread throughout the Mississippi Valley and beyond and then disappeared sometime after De Soto's expedition—he saw it in full flower in the Southeast. Left behind were thousands of temple and burial mounds.

The largest of all the Mississippian centers, and possibly the culture's point of origin, lies across the river from St. Louis at Cahokia Mounds State Park in Illinois. I went there with Nelson A. Reed. A businessman and archeology research associate at Washington University in St. Louis, Nelson specializes in the Mississippian culture. He dropped his duties for the day to guide me around Cahokia.

"Out of perhaps 150 mounds built here 85 remain, the biggest a hundred feet high," Nelson told me. "Inside a wall at its top stood a tall structure, possibly a temple, and many smaller buildings of poles and matting. The site took in five square miles along Cahokia Creek. And it grew here for exactly the reason St. Louis grew over there: It stands above floodwaters and is surrounded by fertile bottomlands, yet it lies close to the junction of three rivers—the Mississippi, Missouri, and Illinois. I think that wherever you find a modern city along the river system, you can bet Indians had a town there too."

Nelson led the way through tall weeds to a small patch planted in seed corn obtained from Sauk and Fox Indians in Iowa and bred back to match the ears the Indians knew in the 14th century. He had brought along a museum piece, a hoe with a flaked stone head. "This tool helped make possible the Mississippian culture in this area," he said as he chopped a few weeds. "Mass-produced from flint, it was strong enough to cut through bottomland sod. My project here is to cultivate Indian corn that is being bred back to what it was in A.D. 850. And of course I'll do the planting and chopping the way the Indians did it. To be really authentic, though, I should get a woman to hoe this patch because I doubt that any self-respecting Indian man would have done it."

Nelson estimated the Cahokian population at about 10,000, by far the largest concentration of pre-Columbian people north of the Valley of Mexico. "Like the people of present-day St. Louis, they carried on a vigorous commerce along the rivers. We have found shells from Florida, mica from North Carolina, and copper from Minnesota. The copper had been cold-worked into repoussé portraits of chieftains or gods. I resist the theory that the Mississippian culture represents only a fifth-rate hand-me-down from Mexico. Although the copperwork has an embarrassingly Mesoamerican look, there are fundamental differences."

To me, the hawk-nosed Indian I had seen in designs pressed on thin copper plates in the City Art Museum of St. Louis looked like the ancient Mexican gods down to fantastic feather headdresses and elaborate costumes. Roughly contemporaneous with the Toltec and Aztec cultures, the Cahokians possibly could have had contacts with those great southern civilizations, and some authorities do trace a connection with the Huastecans of modern Tamaulipas State in Mexico.

Climbing to the top of the highest mound, I could look across the Mississippi and see the white man's ceremonial structure, the Gateway Arch, standing against the sky at St. Louis. Below it, towboats pushed their massed barges along the river that had helped carry the Mississippian culture over what is now the southeastern United States. Some of them hauled corn, basic food of the Indians and their gift to the settlers of the New World. But the barge corn looks far different from the tiny, colored kernels Nelson Reed plants, and the quantities bought, sold, and distributed through St. Louis markets would astound the most imaginative Indian.

*T*HEY ASTOUNDED ME too when I called at the St. Louis offices of Bunge Corporation, a large international grain dealer. Joe Miller, a trader in corn, filled me in on his highly arcane business of buying and selling corn even while it's still growing in the field.

"Nearly half of the corn stays on the farm as feed, but 10 to 15 percent of the crop is shipped abroad, about 600 million bushels in 1970. The bulk of the export goes through New Orleans, arriving there for the most part by Mississippi barge—and for good reason. It costs no more to send a bushel of corn from Illinois all the way to the Gulf by river barge than it does to send a letter across St. Louis. We buy and sell corn in the upper Mississippi Valley and in the Ohio Valley with a gross profit margin of 1½ to 3 percent, so you can see we have no room for error."

In Bunge's boardroom, bells jingled, traders called messages across the floor, and workers came and went on a bewildering tangle of errands.

By long habit, Joe talked with his eyes fixed on the quotation board. "Timing is all-important," he pointed out. "When the market is right, you may sell corn for future delivery even though you haven't bought it yet, or you may buy grain that you know you can't immediately sell, counting on a higher market price when you can sell."

Traders at Bunge also deal in vast quantities of soybeans, a Mississippi lowlands crop that has more than tripled in acreage in the past 20 years.

Dick McWard, the soybean manager, joined us with the news that rain had fallen downriver. "Many factors affect soybean prices," Dick said, "and rain is an important one, depending on how heavy it is, when it falls, and how it affects the crop. Now this rain fell while the plants were putting on beans, and that means farmers can expect a larger crop. With a larger crop, of course, supplies will be greater and prices lower. In simplest terms, that rain is going to shoot down prices, so I'm going to try to sell some beans right now."

His transactions completed, Dick talked about the soybean boom.

"Except for us, only China and Brazil produce sizable soybean crops, and China probably consumes more than 90 percent of its crop. In 1970 Brazil exported 11 million bushels, hardly serious competition for our export of 435 million bushels.

"You can measure a country's standard of living by its meat consumption. Japan, for example, with an increased population and higher family incomes, has shifted some of its limited land from rice and vegetable production to the growing of poultry, hogs, and stall-fed cattle—all eating America's cheap soybeans in the form of meal. You might say that today's young Japanese stand taller than their parents because the Mississippi Valley soybean has upgraded their diet."

In 1969 the United States produced well over a billion bushels of soybeans on 42½ million acres. Every year since 1965 we've added as many as two million acres—more than two Rhode Islands—and most of the new acreage lies in the Mississippi drainage basin. "This year," Dick said, "we may add three million more acres—and we probably should have at least five million to meet the demand."

Fernando Curth, who runs the Bunge company's river operations, spoke up: "Those soybeans may make the Japanese taller, but they make me grayer. In October and November everybody scrambles for barges. We own a hundred of them, but still we carry less than half the grain we export. The storage situation got so desperate four years ago that the city of Hannibal swept the streets and piled them with corn for a week or two. In five or ten years, though, the Corps of Engineers should be maintaining a 12-foot channel from New Orleans to Cairo, Illinois, and we'll be able to use barges half again as big as the standard 60,000-bushel job. That will lighten the downstream problem at least."

Leaving St. Louis, I boarded the towboat *United States*, bound south under the command of Captain Marvin R. Barnes. It was pushing nearly five acres of barges loaded mostly with soybeans. It and its twin the *America* are the most powerful towboats in the world, and a decade ago each cost the Federal Barge Line of St. Louis $2,000,000. Equipped with radar, two-way radio, and a depth recorder, the *United States* takes about five days to push its load the thousand miles or so downstream from St. Louis to New Orleans, and twice as long to return. Traveling on it as a guest is like taking a cruise on a long, seemingly endless lake in an air-conditioned hotel.

Rivermen in Mark Twain's day knew the 180-mile stretch between St. Louis and Cairo as the most treacherous part of the New Orleans run. Sunken rocks and submerged islands that refused to stay put in the swift currents caught and wrecked so many boats in the 50 miles above Cairo that the narrow channel became known as the "Graveyard." According to Twain, a farmer on the Illinois shore "said that twenty-nine steamboats had left their bones strung along within sight from his house." But by 1883, when the author revisited the river, the islands had stuck to one bank or the other, and some of the rocks had been rolled out of the channel by the strong currents. The others were removed so long ago by the Corps of Engineers that Captain Barnes could say that in 42 years on the river he had never heard the name "Graveyard" applied to this stretch.

The afternoon I boarded the *United States* established the all-time heat record for the date, 103° F. The deck force staggered about the steel barges to tighten cables holding them together as a rigid block. Though the men threw all their weight against ratchets armed with cheater bars for greater leverage, little sweat showed, for the humidity was not high that day, and much of the moisture quickly evaporated in the hot breeze.

We stood out into the stream and had scarcely got under way when a haggard deckhand making his first trip — and his last — turned in his resignation. "He picked a tough day to start," the captain said, "but I've worked on that deck under worse sun when I had more years on me than him. If you're going to be a river captain, you usually start on deck, not in the pilothouse as rivermen used to. You can't get mate's papers for 24 months, and if you want pilot's papers it takes another 12 months. And to get them you have to pass the Coast Guard examination. That means, among other things, that you have to draw from memory a map of whatever stretch of the river you plan to work. You have to put in every buoy, point, and sandbar, and all the bank lights by name. But by the time you're ready to take the exam you know all those things."

Captain Barnes played the console of lever controls like an organ. He delicately balanced combinations of speeds on four engines generating 9,000 horsepower, all the while maneuvering the boat's four forward rudders and six backing rudders.

"This kind of tight bend you best make by flanking when you have a tow this size," he said as we approached a deep curve in the river. "You point the barges right at the bank, reverse your engines, and let the fast current along the bank push the barges around the corner. You try to steer by brute strength through there, you going to break apart your 30 barges and scatter them down the river."

Captain Barnes's boat was pushing a tow more than 1,000 feet long, or longer than the *Queen Elizabeth II*. To move the same amount of soybeans or wheat would take 900 freight cars stretching nine miles and pulled by 24 locomotives. A soybean load of that size would sell for about $3,500,000.

Although there's no law requiring towboat pilots to have a Coast Guard license, most companies entrust their costly equipment and valuable cargoes only to men who do. Sometimes, however, a novice takes a turn at the controls of a small vessel. What he doesn't know about the river he has to make up in nerve. With the Coast Guard *Light List* manual he can keep track of where he is, and as long as he stays between the buoys marking the channel and learns by radio from approaching pilots which side he should pass on, he can with luck get where he is headed.

Radar sees through rain, snow, darkness, and light fog, so most of the time boats can keep going day and night with the captain and the pilot taking alternate six-hour shifts. At night the pilot, in the lonely plate-glass control room, swings one of his powerful spotlights across the water to pick up the reflections of the buoys. And every once in a while he runs the beam leisurely along the banks. Often one bank is close by, the other half a mile distant in this section of the river. For while the channel runs more or less down the middle of a straight stretch, the current hugs the outside bank at the bends. As it scours deep, it moves sand toward the opposite bank, building sandbars. And as the current strikes the bank in the bend, it is deflected diagonally across the river, carrying sand as it goes. These "crossings," as they are called, must be cleaned out periodically, and the Corps of Engineers has a fleet of huge dredging machines to vacuum up sand and pump it through pipes to a fill location.

From St. Louis the river drops an average of about four inches a mile all the way to the Gulf. Boats no longer need lock up and down. Rocky hills and sheer cliffs alternate with flatlands, rising sometimes on the east bank, sometimes on the west. Beginning in the St. Louis area, great earthen levees, usually set so far back from the banks that river travelers can't see them, protect lowland stretches.

Rounding a bend, Captain Barnes's tow passed under the highway bridge at Cairo. Trees along the river screen a mile-wide stretch of low-lying farmland. The town itself sits encircled by massive levees and a flood-wall on the point of land where the Ohio and Mississippi join. The mouth of the blue Ohio stretches double the width of the waterway into which it empties, and pours in almost twice as much water as the Mississippi brings from all its tributaries to the north. Some geographers, in fact, consider the Ohio the true mainstream because of its greater volume.

Captain Barnes turned the tow eastward and went up the Ohio a couple of miles to tie up at one of a number of "landing fleets"—anchored barges or groups of pilings—next to Cairo's floodwall. Tugs pushed away some of his barges destined for Sheffield, Alabama, on the Tennessee River. Switching point for barges turning off the Mississippi or coming out of the Ohio, Cairo sees a steady increase in traffic, but gains little profit from it.

River freight is primarily raw material in bulk, and Cairo has few factories needing such cargoes. In recent years, despite its strategic location, the city has attracted no new industries. It has, in fact, lost ground as factories have shrunk, or been moved away. For half a decade Cairo has expended much of its energies and focused most of its attention on the burning buildings, and on the gunfire and other incidents of violence that have flared regularly among black activists, white activists, and police.

Only five miles downstream from Cairo, another river town has shown what makes the difference between moribund little farming towns and prosperous, lively towns with a future. Wickliffe, Kentucky, had long been a static place of about 1,000 people. Many of the young moved to the cities for jobs, leaving behind an aging population.

But in 1966 the town learned that the Westvaco Corporation of New York was considering nearby acreage it had long owned as a possible site for a paper mill. Town officials began to woo the company by offering to issue $80,000,000 in bonds to build the mill. The company agreed to deed the plant site to the city and make rental payments to retire the debt within 25 years. In autumn of 1967 construction began, and three years later the mill began turning out paper. Truckers brought bottomland hardwood logs from Illinois, Kentucky, and Missouri; trains delivered pine logs and chips from as far south as Mississippi. More than $21,000,000 annually in new income began to flow in the area's economic veins. Many townspeople found jobs at the mill, and new housing grew up around Wickliffe as its population quickly increased by 300.

Another 60 miles downstream at New Madrid, Missouri, a group of businessmen with some Federal money and $185,000,000 in tax-free bonds secretly courted Noranda Mines, Ltd., of Canada and persuaded its officers to build the company's projected aluminum reduction plant on 4,000 city-owned acres six miles south on the river. In the fall of 1970 the first shift went to work in the wire and rod mill; the next spring the river bore barges of alumina powder to the new smelter.

In New Madrid, downtown business places are getting a face-lifting, and the sounds of construction — the building of housing and a new generating plant — ring across the riverfront.

On a simmering July day, Larkin Carter of Cairo, Illinois, shades himself with an umbrella. Near his city the Mississippi becomes "Old Man River," entering a realm of southern summers, rich alluvial topsoil, and high levees stretching to the horizon.

Overleaf: Daredevil flier pilots a home-built airplane above St. Louis, "Gateway to the West." The city's symbol, 630-foot Gateway Arch, frames the Eads Bridge ramp in East St. Louis; near the arch stand the Old Cathedral and a columnar high-rise motel. Beyond glowing Busch Memorial Stadium rises the domed Old Courthouse.

At work and at play in St. Louis: S.S. **Admiral** *waits below the Eads Bridge before beginning an evening cruise of 15 miles or so down the river and back. The steel excursion boat—with five decks and room for 4,000 passengers—docks behind craft of another era. The* Goldenrod, *at left, last old-time showboat still on the river, lies moored beside the* Becky Thatcher, *a floating restaurant. Aboard her, a couple (opposite) dines by candlelight. At right, F-4 Phantom fighters take shape at the McDonnell Douglas Corporation, largest industrial employer in the Mississippi Valley.*

Polar bear gobbles a herring,
a reticulated giraffe extends it
tongue for a leaf, and a blac

swan glides serenely on a sunlit pond at the St. Louis Zoo, sanctuary for 853 animal species. Below, a mother and her youngsters walk in fallen leaves near the fenced alligator pit. Each year more than three million visitors explore the 83-acre park.

Visitors to the ornate Brew House of Anheuser-Busch (left) watch as
hops pour into a copper kettle on the ground floor. The dried cones
impart a sharp flavor to the malt solution brewed in tanks on the floor
above. Symbols of the company, the famed Budweiser Clydesdales
(below) pull a brewery wagon at a grape festival in Nauvoo, Illinois.
In a few years the foals at top will replace older horses on the team.

Visitors to Grant's Farm south of St. Louis stroll the courtyard of the Bauernhof, a combination stable, garage, and barn. Buffalo, deer, elk, and other game roam a preserve on the 281-acre tract, once farmed by Ulysses S. Grant and now owned by August A. Busch, Jr.

Carrying nearly twice as much water as the Mississippi, the broad Ohio (at right below) joins the smaller stream to form a mighty river road that flows a thousand miles south to the Gulf. At the confluence lies Cairo, southernmost city in Illinois. Billing itself as the "Gateway to the South" and "Crossroads of the Nation," the racially divided city faces economic collapse despite its strategic location. Nearby, wintering Canada geese soar aloft from the Horseshoe Lake Wildlife Refuge.

Escaping the heat, youngsters romp in a street shower provided by the Cairo Fire Department; the drenched girl above pauses to catch her breath. Below, a puppeteer of the Illinois Arts Council's touring Free Street Theater entertains a child. These pleasures of a summer day belie the violence that often shakes the city.

Cotton, Timber, Miniship

Gilded by a July sunset and rippled by a houseboat's gentle wake, the Mississippi rolls past a park in Memphi

and the "Memphis Sound"

...nnessee. From the Chickasaw Bluff, a man gazes across the water toward Arkansas lowlands.

115

*M*OST GEOGRAPHERS reserve the term "delta" for lands along the river below New Orleans, but many Southerners, with unconscious geological accuracy, refer to the whole 30,000 square miles of bottomland extending southward from Cairo to the Gulf of Mexico as the delta, adding the name of the state for greater precision. From a point almost exactly 1,000 miles from the Gulf, the Mississippi—coursing seaward via a succession of meander belts to either side of its present channel—has deposited ton upon ton of silt and sediment stripped from the upstream drainage basin across a former floodplain 25 to 80 miles wide. So recently has the river laid down this alluvial carpet that Egyptian pyramids built 5,000 years ago antedate most of it by more than two millenniums. The final 70 miles of land thrusting into the present-day Gulf did not exist on the first Christmas Day.

Much of the northern portion of this alluvial plain was shaken to its very bedrock by the New Madrid earthquake, or to be more precise, by the series of quakes that struck the region in 1811 and 1812. An early-day amateur seismologist in Louisville, Kentucky—working with pendulums of varying lengths—recorded and classified 1,874 distinct shocks beginning with the first violent New Madrid upheaval at 2 a.m. on December 16, 1811. A doctor in Ste. Genevieve, on the river below St. Louis, stopped keeping a record after counting 500 tremors. Some major shocks were felt as far away as New Orleans to the south and Detroit, Washington, D. C., and Boston to the northeast.

The quake laid waste New Madrid, toppling houses and trees, rending giant fissures in the earth, and plunging a portion of the riverbank on which the town of 800 stood into the Mississippi. Farther south, Little Prairie—now Caruthersville, Missouri—a settlement of about a hundred families, was also devastated. How many lives were lost no one really knows, but because of the low density of population the number was few, and most who died fell victim to the convulsions of the river.

Geologists say the poorly consolidated alluvial deposits of the region contributed significantly to the cataclysmic ground disturbances that occurred over a 100-by-50-mile area in the vicinity of New Madrid. Precise seismic instruments did not exist in those days, of course, but judging from travelers' tales and the evidence left on the land—like the 65-square-mile Reelfoot Lake in Tennessee created by the tremors—the series of earthquakes may have been the greatest to hit North America in historic times. Of the eight worst shocks, several probably rival in magnitude the Alaska earthquake of Good Friday 1964.

Throughout its length the Mississippi follows a tortuous channel. On the upper river I found that this channel has become fairly well established. But below the juncture with the Ohio the enormous pressure of the combined streams through the centuries has undermined the banks to cut ever-growing loops. Before revetments were used to help restrain the river, currents often slashed shortcuts across the weakest points of these loops, normally near their bases. This process left the lower river framed by long, narrow, horseshoe-shaped lakes called oxbows, old bends of the river cut off by its ceaseless writhing.

The same silt-laden waters that gave birth to the lower river country periodically threaten to drown it. With the arrival of the Ohio's volume, the Mississippi's character changes so drastically that the Corps of Engineers has undertaken the most gigantic earth-moving effort in modern history to keep floodwaters from ravaging that rich basin. An estimated 850,000,000 cubic yards of earth have gone into building the nearly 1,600 miles of levees that stretch along lowlands from Cape Girardeau, Missouri, on the west bank and Cairo on the east to the delta below New Orleans. Even the Great Wall of China cannot quite match the Mississippi's levees for length.

Engineers planned those immense works to contain a theoretical super-flood, one that might occur once in a hundred years. During such a flood, the Ohio would pour into the lower river some five times the volume of the Mississippi and Missouri combined.

I stood on the levee at Wilson, Arkansas, 80 miles south of New Madrid, with Robert E. Lee Wilson III to survey as much as we could see of the 47-square-mile plantation he supervises as president of Lee Wilson & Company. So large is the plantation that if its full acreage were put into row crops like soybeans or cotton, the rows end to end would be long enough to stretch four times around the world at the equator.

The company also operates 18 other enterprises including supermarkets, barber and beauty shops, a construction company, an insurance agency, a drug store, a laundry and dry cleaner, a medical and dental clinic—and even a railroad with one locomotive and two miles of track, the Delta Valley and Southern. Its main buildings surround a small landscaped park in the center of town.

"We run just about every service a farmer needs except a sawmill," said Bob, who lives with his family in a baronial mansion. "And yet the whole thing began when my grandfather set up a sawmill here in 1886. With five to ten feet of topsoil—the world average runs only about seven inches—he had the good sense to send the plow in right behind the saw, turning cutover woods into farmland.

"The river almost took back the riches it gave him, in 1912 and again in 1913. At that sharp bend in the levee you see just north of here, the river broke through—the levee stood only 15 feet high then instead of the present 40 feet. The river swept away his sawmill, the largest in the South, and scattered an immense lumberyard all over Mississippi County. We were picking boards out of treetops and chicken yards for months.

"The levee has never broken since, though I watched floodwaters lap within two feet of the top in 1927 and 1937, and the river spread eight miles wide here."

Grandfather Wilson's sawmill must have had a ravenous appetite, for behind the levee at that latitude the Arkansas delta has been almost entirely cleared for row crops.

"Very few hoes have touched this ground for years," Bob said. "The new mechanized cotton culture eliminates virtually all hand labor."

Bob and I crossed the levee into the batture—the land between levee and riverbank. "This used to be called Last Chance Farm," Bob said, "and the river once ran down the west side. When I was a boy, I'd board the paddle-wheel packet *Kate Adams* right where we're standing and ride four hours to Memphis for the weekend. The packet stopped serving Wilson about 1928—the river had left us two miles inland anyhow. Now we plant a few clearings on Last Chance to milo and corn as quail feed, and we let the weeds grow in the crops because the birds like their seeds too. Not only do these 700 acres support hundreds of game birds for a fall hunt from horseback, but they also carry one of the last packs of timber wolves in the United States."

From Cairo to the Gulf two million acres of batture land lie in a strip sometimes extending as far as 20 miles from either bank—nucleus of a vast forest area covering eight million acres of bottomland and providing one of the world's major sources of commercial hardwoods. A substantial portion grows in the Arkansas and Mississippi battures.

Across the river in Tennessee, I visited a magnificent old-growth batture forest with W. E. Houser, a timber manager for a lumber company, and Sid McKnight, then head of the Southern Hardwoods Research Laboratory at Stoneville, Mississippi.

"You'll never see gum trees this size again," Mr. Houser said. "They take too long to grow. But consider this beauty—80 feet to the first limb, enough tree to make five saw logs 16 feet long."

"I guess at 4,500 board feet in that one tree," Sid said.

We visited a Nuttal oak 135 years old and 150 feet tall and a cherry-bark red oak five feet in diameter.

"And yet we've cut over this tract six times, taking out trees that looked as if they had passed their prime," Mr. Houser said.

"Like all living things, trees have to die," Sid added. "Letting a forest giant go on after it has developed a flat top with horns, showing lowered vitality, wastes forest space and precious time. Without help from the saw, no forest regenerates until it degenerates. But felling ripe trees lets the sun hit the forest floor to nurture seedlings that replace the fallen giant."

On our way out of the woods, I splashed my boots in a water-filled rut to wash off the mud they had collected. Mr. Houser pulled me back and ran a stick through the rut, probing for a possible water moccasin.

"You had luck, my friend," he said. Holding out a hand with a badly crippled finger, he added, "I got careless and lifted a honeysuckle vine from a stump with my bare hand instead of a stick. A copperhead hit me on the finger, and before I could walk out of the woods my arm had swollen to twice normal size and turned black. I had to have a morphine shot every three hours till the fire burned out. And the finger has been useless ever since."

Clouds of mosquitoes worried us more than snakes. Even the deer had been driven from the woods into open farm fields by the insects.

HE WHITE SETTLER came late across the lowlands north of Vicksburg to the Chickasaw Bluff at Memphis, fourth and southernmost of a series of cliffs well known to Frenchmen who camped and hunted there in the late 17th century. When the white settler did come he faced the brutal labor of clearing and draining swamplands to rid the area of malaria, and he brought great coffles of slaves with him from the worn-out fields of the Atlantic seaboard. Today the black man's presence still dominates the delta scene.

During the century and a half after its founding in 1819 by Andrew Jackson and a few cronies, Memphis became the capital of the Arkansas and Mississippi deltas, drawing rural whites and blacks to the big city. And for the blacks Beale Street became the main street of that capital. There a trumpeter named W. C. Handy established himself as the giant of jazz, writing "Memphis Blues," "St. Louis Blues," and "Beale Street Blues" among other classics. In his time music rang up and down the narrow street 24 hours a day.

Randall Johnson, director of planning for the Memphis Housing Authority, drove me along Beale Street and sketched plans to rehabilitate the most shockingly dilapidated historic region I've ever visited.

"First thing tourists want to see in Memphis is Beale Street," Randall said. "You can imagine the disappointment when they see this ramshackle slum. So we're going to spend about 24 million dollars, much of which will be devoted to putting the old street back in the jazz business."

A two-block stretch has been named a National Historic Landmark. There workmen will restore façades and modernize interiors instead of tearing down the buildings that housed the gin mills, pawnshops, bordellos, and hominy grits and chitterlings cafes of Handy's day. Mel O'Brien, architect for the Beale Street Urban Renewal Project, outlined plans.

"Our work extends over 167 acres, centering on the statue of Mr. Handy in Handy Park. From the river bluff to Fourth Street, we'll clear off vehicular traffic for a mall. An elevator will carry passengers down the bluff to a marina and restaurant on the riverfront. In addition to restoring street-level façades, we plan to roof over sidewalks to form a cloistered promenade, something like the Rue de Rivoli in Paris. But ours will be roofed with tinted glass panels to cast a blue light in keeping with the Beale Street project's new name—the Bluelight District."

Mel explained the symbolism of blue light.

"A mixture of white light and black light supposedly makes blue light. We hope white and black visitors and locals can gather to enjoy music and fun from jazz bands playing on outdoor bandstands or at movie houses, restaurants, and nightclubs—whatever kind of business suits the jazzy district Beale Street will become again."

In Memphis a new phase of American popular music has evolved, beginning in 1953 when a young truck driver named Elvis Presley paid a studio four dollars to make a recording. Since then a booming record industry has joined those in Nashville, Tennessee, and Detroit, Michigan, to produce a sound immediately identifiable by its city of origin.

At the offices of Stax, a recording studio on the south side, I sat in a control room and attended a rehearsal of Booker T. and the MG's, a rhythm-and-blues outfit with several million-sellers including "Green Onions." Two young white men, Steve Cropper and Duck Dunn, and two young black men, Al Jackson and Booker T. Jones, tirelessly repeated musical phrases, honing and polishing with inexhaustible patience to make the music sound loose, dionysian, spontaneous, uncontrived.

A red-haired young man, dressed in the vaguely western clothing affected by country and western singers, sat down beside me and introduced himself as Jim Stewart, founder of the studio. He answered the inevitable question about what makes the so-called "Memphis Sound."

"You have an example right here. The two white men come from southern farm backgrounds and cut their guitar picks on country and western; the two black men grew up on rhythm and blues. So you have two musical forms from different cultures expressing the dilemma of the impoverished Southerner, white and black. Put them together, work your heart out to smooth the seams between the two like they're doing, and you've got a *feeling,* a mood. We didn't notice it happening, but the public did, and they hung the name 'Memphis Sound' on it."

On the other side of town stands a monument to another entertainer— St. Jude Children's Research Hospital—the fulfillment of a vow made by a despairing Danny Thomas in 1937 to the patron saint of hopeless causes. Fearing that his stage career had ended before it was well launched, he swore to build a shrine if he ever found his way in life. And Thomas remembered the oath after he became famous. On the advice of Samuel Cardinal Stritch, then in Chicago but originally a parish priest in Memphis, he came to the Mississippi riverbank in Tennessee. There, he decided, the world needed a research center to attack cancer—particularly leukemia— and muscular dystrophy and extreme malnutrition among children.

As a Lebanese-American, Thomas dragooned the American community of Lebanese, Syrians, and others to support his hospital. Today teenagers of all origins solicit funds, Hollywood stars come to Memphis to put on a benefit show, Thomas sponsors a golf tournament, and the U. S. Public Health Service chips in, but the Lebanese and Syrian citizens of the United States continue to hold the hospital as their favorite charity. No patient pays for treatment or drugs at St. Jude's.

When Dr. Donald Pinkel took over as medical director of the uncompleted hospital in 1961, he brought with him a background of years of research in quest of a cure for leukemia.

"The conventional wisdom of medicine then and now said I was wasting my time. Look here in the latest, the 1969, edition of the doctor's *Handbook of Pediatrics*."

Under *Leukemia*, the book read:

"There is no cure for leukemia; treatment is directed at prolonging life and relieving symptoms."

"There you see why I never use a textbook to guide me."

"But surely the book has it right about the cure rate," I protested.

"Of 41 previously untreated cases of leukemia we treated between 1962 and 1965, seven have been taken off all treatment and remain free of leukemia. In a study from 1967 to 1968 we treated 34 patients. Of these 21 have remained free of the disease for two and a half to three years. Previously, the majority of children who passed two years free of leukemia became five-year cures. If this group has the same experience—and I can't think why it shouldn't—we can expect a five-year cure rate of 50 percent. That's not bad for an incurable disease."

Once the world's greatest cotton market, Front Street in Memphis has fallen on hard times—complex Federal farm legislation, focusing on strict acreage controls, has overthrown historic methods of bringing cotton to market. But Memphis goes on booming, supported by an industrial diversification providentially undertaken before shrinkage of the cotton mart. On its bluffs the city has mounted a skyline of towering buildings looking over the vast alluvial empire to the south and west—the fertile plain that has supported the Memphis marketplace for 150 years.

Below Memphis in the battures of the lower Mississippi and its tributaries pioneer cottonwood forests have been planted. Fastest-growing tree in North America, the cottonwood thrives in wet mineral soil on lands subject to river overflow, and it tolerates frequent flooding. The timber is light and tough, and large sections are clear of knots. Cutting for pulpwood can begin in as little as four years, and lumber and veneer logs can be cut in 14. Mature cottonwood provides wood for furniture frames and architectural trim as well as for veneer. Pulpwood from the earlier cut is used in the making of a fine paper for photographic reproductions, and in the manufacture of toothpicks and matches. Anticipating future needs, some large paper companies have planted thousands of acres in trees.

Frank Shropshire, a U. S. Forest Service hardwoods specialist, took me on a tour of commercial tree plantations in the Arkansas and Mississippi batture lands, a hundred miles or so south of Memphis.

While we angled across a turbulent swollen river in a boat that persisted in breaking down and drifting against snags, he preached the forester's gospel.

"With patience a man can make more farming trees than he can raising soybeans on bottomlands subject to flooding during the growing season. The cottonwoods continue to grow because their tops stay above high-water level. In a depressed market, the soybean grower may have to store his crop, but the tree farmer can let his crop grow and sell bigger trees for more money in a better year."

Frank conceded that high interest rates on the $110 it takes to plant an acre to trees could try the patience of a farmer who must wait four years for a first profitable thinning for pulpwood.

"But game multiplies wildly in a mixed cottonwood and pecan stand. Deer browse on twigs, and turkeys eat insects; both need 15 percent mast, or fallen nuts, in their diet for reproduction. Pecans sheltered by cottonwoods litter the ground with the protein wildlife needs. And the farmer leases the land to hunters for an additional income while he waits for the dollars to grow on trees. Nearly every square foot of forested batture in Arkansas and Mississippi brings in added revenue from hunting clubs."

Through its state offices the United States Forest Service offers technical assistance and some monetary support to growers of cottonwood trees. It has also selected and propagated certain species for timber production in the lower Mississippi Valley. The new stock will be ready for planting within two years.

We stepped ashore on Georgetown Towhead on the Arkansas bank, and Frank let me walk ahead alone so I could turn up game. Within a quarter of a mile I saw a deer, a black snake, an armadillo, lizards, and a dozen doves dusting themselves in the road. Quail called all about and suddenly a covey burst from high grass beside the path. A flock of turkeys took off from a roost on one side of the road and glided on silent wings into the dark forest on the river side.

Disk harrows had cultivated the plantation's saplings to give them a lift over the first year in the field. A bulldozer had cleared scrub growth and piled it around the field as a brush fence against the deer that prefer yearling cottonwood top leaves to any other salad. But the bulldozer hadn't pushed hard enough, for a bevy of does briefly interrupted their browsing to stare at us with a limpid, curious gaze. We had to chase them back over the fence and into the woods.

On the other side of the river at Catfish Point, I toured the levee with Robert Clanton, a graduate student in wildlife management studying the wild turkeys of the batture. Deer grazed under open sky, mixing freely with horse herds. Two deer at the foot of the levee raced our four-wheel-drive pickup truck like a pair of collies. "Turkey and deer population on this point stand just about at top capacity for the habitat," Bob said. "Except for the occasional wild dog, there are few predators to prey on large game species. The rare cougar, red wolf, bear, or coyote soon gets shot by a sportsman. So nothing but hard hunting or disease can thin the herds and flocks to healthy numbers."

Within minutes we found a young buck with buttons for antlers whose back had been broken, probably by a car. Its hindquarters paralyzed, the stricken deer painfully tried to drag itself to the protection of the forested batture. Protruding ribs showed that the animal had been making that endless journey for perhaps a week, proving Bob right about predators. Had they been present in sufficient numbers they would have done the job of a warden's merciful shot. State wildlife specialists, soon after my visit, discovered epidemic lungworm infestations of deer herds in two Mississippi River counties farther south and placed the blame on overpopulation and a lack of predators.

*T*HOUGH I moved to Greenville just after World War II, I have known the river even longer. I first frequented its banks in college days when I was courting an Arkansas girl and we trooped with other youngsters to the landing at Arkansas City for an all-night dance aboard the *Senator* or the *President*, transient pleasure packets. The streets echoed to youthful laughter, and Arkansas City ran with vigorous sap, or so it seemed to me. But for the townspeople no amount of boat-night revelry could disguise the fact that Arkansas City, home to 10,000 in its heyday, was dying—a casualty of the great flood of 1927 that had washed over it more than a decade before.

Then one spring the river slithered sideways, leaving a dwindling village of vacant buildings with only courthouse business to keep alive a flickering spirit. Two miles east the life-giving and life-taking river rolls capriciously along.

Just below Greenville the Mississippi pours out of a sharp bend and aims its full force at the bridge carrying U. S. Highway 82 traffic across the river. In one pilothouse where I rode as a guest, I listened as the captain upbraided the pilot for stalling on his watch to throw the passing of the bridge into his superior's lap.

Boatmen have reason to fear that bridge and the fierce current beneath it. During an ice storm on March 4, 1948, the towboat *Natchez* hit a pier on the Arkansas side and rolled over. I remember the date because I was creeping home across the ice-glazed bridge after having a first glimpse of my daughter, just born in Lake Village, Arkansas, when the *Natchez* hit below me. I stood until midnight on the windy riverbank watching helplessly as boats swept the river with lights searching for survivors. Miraculously, 13 of the crew of 26 lived through that long night.

Similarly savage currents once plagued Greenville, but just before World War II the Corps of Engineers closed off the upstream end of the channel running down the eastern side of Archer Island, across from the city, thus halting a remorseless chewing away of the downtown business district. The lower end of the channel remains open and dredged, making Greenville a first-rate slack-water port supporting a huge towboat fleet, building yards for boats and barges, and marine repair shops.

And with at least 16 feet of water in the channel 11 months of the year, a Greek flag line already numbering 32 miniships — built in Japan especially for river and saltwater trade — has begun operating out of Greenville, making it a seaport 530 miles upriver from the ocean. The ships calling there have hinged masts to slide under bridges on the Atchafalaya shortcut from below Natchez to the Gulf, so they can save 175 miles or a full day's travel upstream and also bypass congested coastal ports.

Milton Barschdorf, a West Pointer who retired as district engineer at Vicksburg for the Corps of Engineers to operate Greenville's port, took me on a tour of one of the miniships. Carrying cargo in containers eight feet square by 20 feet long, the ships out of Greenville run to Costa Rica and back with way-stops in the Caribbean.

"River ports now make the fifth coast after the Atlantic, the Pacific, the Great Lakes, and the Gulf," Milton said. "With the new containers, and barges designed to be lifted straight aboard ocean-going ships, every river port can become a seaport. We have a full-time customs man here, but any river port can get one for a special cargo by paying per diem wages."

Checking the manifest, I found that the *Mini Luck,* a 215-foot vessel with a 3,100-ton capacity, was taking on steel billets and popcorn for Costa Rica, oats for Panama, rice for Jamaica, insulation for Venezuela, cottonseed, soybean meal, vetch seed, saws, sunflower seed, and high-density cotton bales for scattered Caribbean ports. The ship would be back in five weeks with a cargo of logs and rubber tires of an American trademark made in Costa Rica.

So the little backwoods town where, between voyages abroad, I rusticate under pecan trees, has become a port opening on the salt seas.

At night when the whistles moan in the channel and lights sweep the sky, I'll now suffer the added poignancy of knowing the crew of that craft may be going to islands where palm fronds rattle under the trade winds and flying fish skip across foaming wave crests.

Nostalgic remnant of another time, the stern-wheeler Delta Queen *churns downriver from Memphis toward Vicksburg on an autumn cruise. Launched in 1926, she survives as the last overnight passenger steamboat still in service on the Mississippi River.*

Cotton thrives in alluvial loam near Wilson, Arkansas. Spraying with defoliants (above) strips leaves from plants to make picking easier (left). President of Lee Wilson & Company, Robert E. Lee Wilson III (far right, with wife Mildred and daughters Midge, standing, and Diana) controls 30,000 acres of cropland; the Wilson cotton gin (right) processes 5,000 bales a year.

Floodlit arrival of Queen Patte Quinlen and the royal court at the Ceremonial Barge (triple
exposure above) opens the 1970 Memphis Cotton Carnival. For a festive week each May,

*marching bands fill the streets, balloons bob, and
young curbside revelers watch elaborate parades.*

*Overleaf: Lightning rips the sky over Memphis,
metropolitan center of the mid-South. In a time
exposure, automobile lights streak Riverside Drive
along the Mississippi River. Luring settlers
here in 1819, a land advertisement noted that
Memphis afforded a "situation sufficiently high,
dry, level, and extensive, together with a rich
surrounding country competent to support it."*

Onetime jazz and gambling mecca, shabby Beale Street shows no trace of its colorful past (opposite). Memphis plans complete renovation of this historic neighborhood, where W. C. Handy composed "Memphis Blues" in 1911 and "St. Louis Blues" in 1914. Above, guitarists improvise in a riverside park. At a Stax recording studio, versatile musician Isaac Hayes vocalizes the "Memphis Sound."

"The greatest killer of children is poverty," says Dr. Donald Pinkel, Medical Director of St. Jude Children's Research Hospital in Memphis (below). The center, founded to study and treat childhood diseases, cooperates with Memphis Area Project-South, a community self-help organization; working in a joint nutrition program, Sister Mary Anne of St. Jude's gives advice on child care to a young ghetto mother (right).

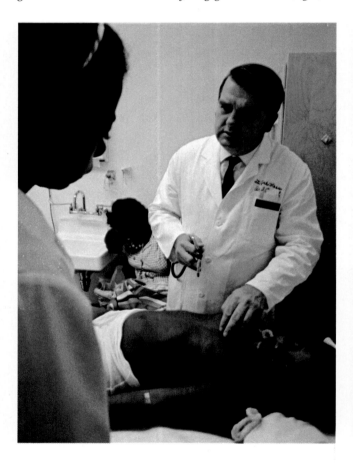

In a natural stand of cottonwood trees at Huntington Point, Mississippi,
Verranel Chism (opposite) cuts logs for shipment to the Chicago Mill
and Lumber Company in nearby Greenville. Growing in a seasonally
flooded area, the trees mature faster than those on levee-protected
ground; cultivated stands yield pulpwood in four years, lumber in four-
teen. Joe Bridges (above) operates a "skidder" that moves and stacks
logs for loading onto Greenville-bound trucks. At the mill, Thompson
Pruitt supervises the initial sawing of logs for boxes and furniture.

Washed by summer rain, the stately columns of Windsor evoke vanished magnificence in Mississippi. Spared in t

vil War, the plantation house near Port Gibson burned in 1890, set ablaze by a cigarette.

*O*NCE, no region exceeded the State of Mississippi in fervor of patriotic celebration on Independence Day. But on July 4, 1863, the fortress city of Vicksburg, whose majestic bluffs commanded the river, fell to Federal troops after a year of maneuvering culminated by a 47-day siege. The Mississippi River became a Union stream. For the South it became a water barrier that split the Confederacy in two, isolating Texas, Arkansas, most of Louisiana, and partisans in Missouri and the Western territories. And for 82 years thereafter on Independence Day, many Vicksburgers ignored the event, staying at home or going about their daily routine.

Then in 1945, in a wave of patriotic pride after the surrender of Nazi Germany, Vicksburg resumed the observance of July 4. I photographed the celebration two years later when Gen. Dwight D. Eisenhower appeared as speaker. I marveled as the man who commanded all the Allied World War II forces in Europe used his personal magic and oratory to inspire a spirit of brotherhood on the anniversary of American independence.

Nevertheless, the siege still has its impact on life in Vicksburg. A girdle of forts and trenches half a mile wide and nine miles long, now enshrined in a United States national park, has long confined the city to its small area at the edge of the river bluff. In recent years, however, the National Park Service has turned over to the city a new bypass road and 154 acres of land in the southern part of the fortifications for development of such non-commercial projects as parks, playgrounds, and schools.

When Maj. Gen. Ulysses S. Grant found that invasion of the city over bluffs or swamps was impractical, and that bombarding by river gunboats did not bring surrender, he landed his troops on low riverbanks to the south. In the course of two months his army marched inland, cut the rail-road, and attacked from the land side. I visited that crescent-shaped battle-field of slopes, deep ravines, and small meadows, marked with some 500 stone memorials.

More than any other Civil War battlefield, Vicksburg gives me a clear impression of the problems of terrain both sides faced, and some of the tactical solutions each devised. Inside the Louisiana Redan, I peered over the parapet and down the hill at the markers climbing the steep slopes. They showed the farthest advance of Union troops during a mas-sive frontal attack so costly and unsuccessful that Grant gave up such tactics and settled down to the siege.

I tried charging up the Confederate slope myself. Although I ran without the weight of gun and ammunition and no felled trees bristling with sharpened limbs lay in my way, I gave out, spent, short of the lip of the redan. I recalled as I lay there panting that some 3,200 Union dead and wounded littered that same ground during a single assault.

With the defeat at Vicksburg, the Confederacy suffered a fatal wound, but it agonized two years more before dying.

Shortly after the war ended in April 1865, the city played a role in another tragedy—the worst steamboat disaster in history. The side-wheeler *Sultana*, bound from New Orleans to Cincinnati, tied up at Vicksburg for boiler repair. Although his passenger list was limited to 376, the captain allowed some 2,000 Union troops newly released from Confederate prisons to pack aboard. At 2 a.m. on April 27, as the *Sultana* toiled against the spring current just above Memphis, one of her four boilers exploded. Within 20 minutes the boat burned to the waterline. Men strong enough to survive the infamous prison at Andersonville, Georgia, were swept away by the flooding river. The death toll, according to several accounts, exceeded 1,500, rivaling that of the *Titanic*.

A park overlook at the edge of the 200-foot Vicksburg bluff gives visitors a sweeping view of the loop of river where Union gunboats lay while bombarding the city. But the loop is no longer part of the Mississippi. Thirteen years after Vicksburg surrendered, the river cut across the loop's neck and left the city isolated on an oxbow lake rapidly silting up at both ends, doing naturally what Grant's engineers had tried and failed to do before the siege. For years, stranded Vicksburg appealed to the Government for help. Finally the Engineers came up with a solution. In 1904 they finished digging a nine-mile-long canal north from the Vicksburg arm of the loop to the Yazoo River, dammed off the Yazoo from the Mississippi, and turned its waters into the canal. Dredging the lower end of the oxbow opened a route to the Mississippi for Vicksburg, and the current of the Yazoo has kept it scoured since. The comparatively slack water of the channel makes a superb harbor, and Vicksburg has now pulled ahead of Greenville as first in the State of Mississippi in tonnage of soybeans, steel, lumber, grain, gravel, and petroleum moved on the river. A new and expanding harbor industrial area boasts factories and boatyards.

But the biggest work force in the Vicksburg area labors for the Corps of Engineers—some 680 in its District Office, 800 at its Waterways Experiment Station, and 200 for the Mississippi River Commission. The Commission directs a July-to-December force of about 2,500 along the lower river; roughly a third of the men work in the Vicksburg area. They dredge crossings, grade banks, and put together and lay concrete mats on crumbling banks. Hundreds more work for private employers under contract to the Engineers, carrying on the ceaseless battle to control the river.

Since 1930, when the Engineers began working on flood control and river navigation, the Waterways Experiment Station, world's largest hydraulic laboratory, has tested with exact models many projects or structures proposed for America's inland waterways. The models, as well as a test laboratory for soil mechanics, are in a dozen or so hangarlike buildings south of Vicksburg. Until 1969, when its work was completed and recorded on computer tapes, a model of the lower Mississippi laid out on a 200-acre field near Jackson, Mississippi, tested flood-control works between Hannibal and Baton Rouge and along the Missouri, Ohio, and Atchafalaya.

Where cotton was once king, from Vicksburg downriver to Natchez, the country supported an elegant plantation aristocracy. Throughout the backwoods today, many superb examples of antebellum architecture stand deserted, visited only by an occasional artist, photographer, or careless hobo. Many manors have burned; others molder among pine trees, or live oak and cypress hung in Spanish moss. Fortunately, a few magnificent mansions remain as gracious homes, or have been restored.

One, Windsor, was destroyed by fire and became an abandoned ruin in a lonely clearing of the dank wood near Port Gibson, Mississippi. Today the 22 columns, standing five stories high and topped with cast-iron Corinthian capitals, mutely mark where the countryside's most imposing mansion stood until it burned in 1890. By chance, I met the builder's namesake and grandson, who died only months after telling me Windsor's story.

"Grandfather had just finished the building on a 2,000-acre plantation when the Civil War broke out," the venerable Smith Daniell IV recalled. "Later, as Grant landed his troops near Bruinsburg just up the river, he mistook some furniture set out on the third-floor veranda for soldiers, and thought that the building was a fort. It took all of Grandmother's considerable persuasive power to keep the general from burning the house.

"But it did burn 27 years later, in 1890. When I was about five years old we had a house party for a number of young ladies, and naturally all the eligible bachelors in the countryside came to call. Some were smoking cigarettes, a new fad at the time, and one of them, I'm told, carelessly tossed aside a stub. The place was in flames and the roof falling in within minutes. There was nothing anyone could do."

From the riverbank nearby, where Grant landed to take Vicksburg from the rear, I traveled the same sunken road he had followed. The soil in this area is loess, a fine brownish loam deposited by the winds of the Ice Age. It has the peculiar quality of being able to stand in sheer walls without crumbling. In this lonely trench, trees meet overhead and Spanish moss hangs down into the gloom. The air carries the punky smell of forest floor. I recalled that several of Grant's young Union officers wrote letters home to describe their nervousness when they moved down that road; they feared an ambush from the high wooded banks, but the Rebels let their chance slip and the Union force emerged unharmed.

The Natchez Trace, another sunken road and the most famous in America, ran nearby through Port Gibson, on its way from Natchez to Nashville, five hundred miles northeast. Southbound settlers in the early 1800's walked the Trace, already worn deep through centuries of trampling by deer, bison, Indians, and traders. Until the days when steamboats offered easy rides back home, farmers from the Ohio Valley rafted their produce downstream, sold it, raftwood and all, and went home by foot or on horseback along the Natchez Trace.

At Natchez, the riverboatmen and farmers equipped themselves for the long overland journey. Many of them bolstered their courage against the murderous thieves on the Trace with a drunken visit to the saloons, gambling houses, and brothels of Natchez-Under-the-Hill. On a ledge at the foot of a 200-foot loess bluff below Natchez City, the assembled riffraff of the river and their patrons clamored through the streets until dawn with dancing and revelry, gouging matches and knife fights.

Little remains of that turbulent Gomorrah today, for since the 1930's, when the Corps of Engineers cut off a loop upstream, the river currents at Natchez have been faster and stronger, battering harder than ever at the ledge and carrying away all but half a dozen dilapidated red brick buildings. When I last visited under the hill I was startled by a basso voice booming from one of the old buildings. A tobacco-chewing elder clumped into the sunshine and introduced himself as Marion Casey "Babe" Morris. Once a river sailor and sawmill hand, and one of the last residents under the hill, Babe had lived there most of his 75 years. He had worked as a roustabout on a ferry that crossed to Vidalia, Louisiana, and he remembered well the steam packets that carried freight between Natchez and the world as recently as the 1940's.

"The stern-wheeler *David Swain* hit a stump right out there and sank in the '30's," he said. "And the absolutely last one was the *Tennessee Belle* that burned in 1942 near Natchez Island just out of sight downstream. All they saved was the whistle. Luckily, the crew was able to step ashore before she sank and walk back to town in dry shoes. They sat around here for a while toasting their luck in good corn whiskey, then picked up their whistle and went home. It marked the end of an era."

Only the great bridge spanning the Mississippi, and an indistinct line of buildings on the high bluff of the east bank, tell the boat traveler that he is passing Natchez. Once the biggest port on the Mississippi between New Orleans and the Ohio River, and a center of sumptuous living, Natchez declined after the Civil War, crippled by the boll weevil and the railroads. Only since about 1940 has it begun to stir again. In the ten years after 1960 I watched the pace accelerate rapidly, as the town added a number of suburbs and three large shopping centers. Oil and natural gas discovered in quantity in local fields, a good supply of lumber and pulpwood, a mechanized new port behind the levee—all keep drawing plants to its industrial parks.

What draws visitors, I learned, is the re-created elegance of Natchez's antebellum days. "People always want to come back to Natchez. We've boomed economically, but we haven't gone hustle-bustle modern. With 40 or so old mansions right in Natchez, we would hardly dare go garish,"

Mayor Tony Byrne pointed out. In fact, the ladies of the town, who since the early 1930's have led in the restoration of old homes, have enlisted downtown merchants in a campaign to refurbish old Natchez into a living museum of pre-Civil War days.

For a month beginning in early March, about 30 of the mansions are opened to visitors making the "Natchez Pilgrimage." Proceeds go for restoring more buildings belonging to Natchez's romantic past. During the Pilgrimage in 1969, ladies in period costumes greeted at least 35,000 visitors at such places as The Briars, home of beautiful Varina Howell and scene of her marriage to Jefferson Davis, later President of the Confederacy; Rosalie, headquarters for Federal officers during the years of Union occupation; and Hope Farm, once the residence of a Spanish governor. Several houses rotate a year-round schedule of openings.

*D*own by the port of Natchez, life aboard the Coast Guard buoy tender *Chena* follows a rougher style for men who keep river traffic moving between Natchez and Baton Rouge. Master Chief Boatswain's Mate N. R. Rowell, a veteran of 20 years on the river, and his crew of 14 sleep and eat on the Mississippi most of the time while they tend 175 channel buoys and 101 lights that flash on the banks. "The river is carrying big waves of sand on the bottom, and the channel moves, you know," Chief Rowell explained. "In high water, boats and barges don't have much trouble. But when the river falls, we have to find out where the channel is and move the buoys to mark its limits." The Corps of Engineers used to do this work, but the Coast Guard took over six years ago, operating seven tenders between Cairo and New Orleans.

Years ago, the bank lights were kerosene lanterns hanging on poles or trees, and lamplighters went by boat every day or so to keep them filled. But battery-powered blinkers now sit on top of 20-foot steel towers. "Last time we checked them," Chief Rowell said, "five towers had caved into the river. We have to set them back up and chop out an acre or so of willows around them so the pilots can see them. And any time you set foot on those banks, you're going to get poison ivy. I just had to transfer a man because he suffered so bad with a chronic case of ivy poisoning."

Once in a while a man falls overboard, and even though he's wearing a life jacket as required by regulations, he can drown if he gets caught in an eddy or swift current. "We have lifeboat drill so we can pick up a man within three minutes," Chief Rowell said. "Believe me, I respect that river."

Some 50 miles south of Natchez stands one of two structures on the west bank that have kept the restless Mississippi from running off to a different channel. Just visible from the river is a gate that controls the amount of water allowed to flow out of the Mississippi and through a channel to the Red-Atchafalaya river system six miles west. On down the river another five miles, the second structure dams off Old River, except for a lock big enough for small ocean vessels using the Atchafalaya to bypass New Orleans and save mileage to Natchez, Vicksburg, or Greenville.

In the early 1950's, the Engineers warned that each year more and more of the Mississippi's waters were running out through Old River to the narrow Red-Atchafalaya rivers, following a steeper, shorter path to the sea. Gradually the increased volume was cutting the Atchafalaya wider and deeper, so that by 1975 its capture of the Mississippi would be inevitable. Thus the Atchafalaya would become the main watercourse. Baton Rouge and New Orleans would be stranded on a quiet stream, and the 115 miles along the Atchafalaya to the Gulf would require a huge flood-control investment. To avert such a disaster, a channel with flow-control gates at its juncture with the Mississippi was built to replace Old River. At either normal or flood stage, the channel lets about 25 percent of the Mississippi's volume through to the Atchafalaya.

This control point will also play an important role when the once-a-century superflood moves toward Baton Rouge and New Orleans. Flood-waters will surge through the channel, swelling the Atchafalaya and piling up in the Red River backwater area. Flowing westward, the floodwaters will overtop and breach a levee built to give way, then pour into the six-mile-wide West Atchafalaya Floodway, an area of soybean growing, cattle grazing, forest, and wilderness. Superflood volume on the Mississippi will be further reduced by the Morganza Floodway, some 35 miles below the Old River channel. Still more water will be released into the Gulf through the Bonnet Carre Spillway and Lake Pontchartrain.

Water carried by the Atchafalaya system will converge in the southern half of the Atchafalaya Basin Floodway. Many outflowing streams and bayous in this swampy area have been cut off to hold the river in a centralized, deepened channel. This has caused some fish and wildlife to die as their supply of replenishing overflow water has become uncertain. The changing ecology alarms conservationists; they hope studies now under way will lead to preserving some of the lower basin in its natural state, a wilderness paradise for fishing and hunting.

I toured the basin's swampland by boat with then district forester Jewel L. Willis. He poled us along a bayou, its banks crowded with willow, cottonwood, sycamore, and sweet gum trees. In swamps bounding the bayou grew cypresses and tupelo gums. At the village of Bayou Geneve, I saw several men of mixed Indian features, and I was reminded that many Chitimacha Indians once inhabited these swamps. Only a few retain their tribal identity, living not far away on the great Bayou Teche.

Leaving the boat to walk the occasional ridge, I stepped high and watched for snakes. But Jewel strode on. "I used to stop and kill as many as 30 moccasins a day, but I got to be like the old-time lumbermen. I just ignore them."

Sportsmen along the Mississippi from Memphis to Baton Rouge have within easy reach at least one oxbow lake or stream or bayou wilderness for their pleasure. But from Baton Rouge south there are no oxbows, and the Mississippi becomes even more dangerous than it is farther north, with big boats and barges, swift currents, and industries dropping in pollutants. So Baton Rouge and New Orleans fishermen take their tackle up to the nearest oxbows: False River, Old River, Lake Concordia at Natchez, and Lake St. John and Lake Bruin some miles beyond.

Bob Dennie, associate editor of the *Louisiana Conservationist* magazine in New Orleans, goes to Old River. "It's on the Mississippi side of the levee, still connected to the big river," he said. "One side is lined with fishermen's camps. I rent a boat and go across to the wild side where willows stand along the edge. Fish hide there in the shady water. In no time I can usually catch a mess of crappie, bream, bass, and catfish."

Catfish fillets sell to restaurants for 90 cents a pound, and fishermen put out trotlines to catch a string at a time. "They may bait with worms, but mostly they use cheese or Ivory soap. Catfish smell with their whiskers, and for some reason when they get a whiff of that soap, they come straight to the hook. Dealers buy it by the barrel just for bait," Bob said.

During the past few years, catfish farming has attracted scores of enterprising men who with luck can gross up to $6,000 in a year by stocking a five- or six-acre pond with fingerlings, then harvesting the catfish when they reach about a pound in weight. And demand is still double production.

O N MY WAY down the river to Baton Rouge, I noticed that wherever power lines cut a swath through hardwood forests, nearly all the poles were wrapped in wire mesh. Robert L. Rumsey, wildlife biologist with the U. S. Forest Service at Pineville, Louisiana, explained the reason for such extraordinary coverings — woodpeckers. "The birds love to peck big holes for nests in creosoted poles," he told me, "and it weakens the poles and exposes their interiors to decay. Nobody knows for sure why woodpeckers prefer them to trees, but sometimes it seems to me the more unpleasant and smelly a pole may be from creosote, the better the birds like it."

They favor pecking on the upper portions of the poles, and since 1948 power-company crews have wrapped the top three-fourths in wire mesh, mostly before putting the poles up. Costs can run $50 a pole and it's about 95 percent effective, although as I watched, a woodpecker emerged from a hole he had chopped right through the wire. Power companies keep looking for a completely effective deterrent, and currently ten companies are financing a Forest Service project to find better repellents.

"Actually, we're working as much for the woodpeckers as for the power companies," Bob said, "for nests in newly creosoted poles are unsuccessful. If the eggs hatch at all, the naked young soon die. The problem plagues the Gulf Coast area especially, but wherever there are power poles in or near hardwood forests — whether in Michigan, Pennsylvania, Japan, or Czechoslovakia—the power companies have to work hard to outwit the birds."

On the north side of Baton Rouge, overlooking the Mississippi from Scott's Bluff, lies the campus of Southern University. Established in 1914, the school has nearly 8,000 students in Baton Rouge and 3,000 others in Shreveport and New Orleans. Its students sport a dazzling display of dashikis—colorful baggy shirts with long, wide sleeves—and Afro coiffures. But no one was more dazzling than Alvin Batiste, who turned out to be not a student but a professor, founder and head of the newly created Jazz Institute and third among clarinetists of the world in a 1970 poll, composer for "Cannonball" Adderley and onetime baritone sax with Ray Charles. We settled down to talk in one of his classrooms, cluttered with speakers, tape recorders, sheet music, all the tools found in any jazz recording studio.

The curriculum includes courses in jazz history, improvisation, and ensemble, with others planned in arranging, voice, and theater work.

"But the most important new course will be in the business side of music," Alvin said. "When I was coming up in New Orleans, we had to learn the hard way, in low-life nightclubs, surrounded by dope, prostitution, and scheming managers. Even a really sharp musician has to survive financially to develop his art. I don't want the talented kids hurt by the naïve idea that just being good insures success."

To explain the difference between serious jazz and commercial pop music, Alvin gave me a lecture so rich in pentatonic scales, microtones, multi-ethnic trends, innovative thrusts, and Afro-Brazilian overlays that I was left far behind. But when he flipped on a tape and played some jazz improvisations his students had just recorded, I dug it well enough. "About a hundred kids are taking jazz courses, and nine are seriously studying jazz. They're very promising. I hope they stay in the South and organize bands—open up new opportunities for good musicians down here where jazz was born," Alvin said.

The major road into Baton Rouge from the north is called Scenic Highway and runs for some blocks beside three of the big plants and many smaller ones that make up one of the greatest petrochemical manufacturing complexes in the world. Baton Rouge lies amid the highly productive oil fields of Louisiana, Mississippi, and Texas. Pipelines from these areas feed the crude oil into the Baton Rouge plants, where hundreds of products are turned out—gasoline, jet fuel, lubricants, waxes, kerosene, naphtha. And the area's industry, of course, pours millions into the community, $375,000,000 in payrolls in 1970.

One current project shared by members of the industrial complex is to preserve the ecology of the Mississippi River. More than a million and a half people in communities between Baton Rouge and New Orleans take their drinking water from the Mississippi, and industries employ much money and manpower to try to keep the river clean. During my visit, however, Murray Stein, an enforcement officer for the Federal Environmental Protection Agency, reported that industry was spilling 4,800 pounds of lead and 80 pounds of arsenic daily into the Mississippi between the two cities. But help may be on the way.

Peter Miller of Rollins-Purle, Inc., drove me to the company's regional industrial-pollution control plant near the northern city limits. The heart of the plant is a huge incinerator which operates at temperatures up to 3,000° Fahrenheit with the capacity to break down virtually any waste from hydrocarbons to chlorine. The plant also treats industrial wastes through biological degrading and chemical reaction. It can handle about 250,000 gallons daily through these three methods of treatment. The only residues are inert ash, saline water, and a harmless mixture of steam and carbon dioxide which comes from the incinerator stack.

"No single industry finds it feasible to build its own plant," Pete said. "Ours operates around the clock on wastes collected by tank truck from a radius of 75 miles. At our present capacity, the concentrated pollutants we treat would be sufficient to contaminate nearly 38 billion gallons of Mississippi River daily if dumped into the stream."

Dale Givens, a biologist for the Division of Water Pollution Control of the Louisiana Wildlife and Fisheries Commission, took me on a tour of the industrial waterfront.

In back eddies we saw swarms of *Gambusia* fingerlings devouring hordes of mosquito larvae, an occasional mullet jumping, and spotted gars swimming about. The river bottom had not died; indeed, it was flourishing all too abundantly, its algae overfertilized by discharges high in phosphates.

"But you mustn't exaggerate the extent that river pollution has reached here," he cautioned. "A minimum of 100,000 cubic feet of Mississippi River water flows by every second. Vertical mixing takes place almost immediately and lateral mixing in 14 miles. By that point, it takes incredibly delicate instruments to detect the discharge from Baton Rouge industry."

Beginning at Baton Rouge, the river, now half a mile wide, rolls south between unbroken bankside levees. Behind them stretches flat farmland marked occasionally by the buildings and smokestacks of industry— about a hundred plants, with a total value of some four billion dollars, lie scattered along the 130 miles to New Orleans. During our cruise, Dale and I hailed sailors on the decks of ships flying the flags of Yugoslavia, Japan, Liberia, Greece, Norway, Mexico, and West Germany. Ocean tides affect the Mississippi faintly here, and I felt the first tug of the open sea urging me toward the river's mouth and a captivating city, New Orleans.

Miniature Mississippi winds past visitors to the Army's Waterways Experiment Station outside Vicksburg. The two-acre lower river model, forerunner of a 200-acre installation near Jackson, demonstrates flood-control and water-diversion measures.

Armored with hard, diamond-shaped scales, an eight-foot alligator gar glides near the surface of the Mississippi; another chases a young blue catfish. Largest fish in the river, gars sometimes grow ten feet long. Scaleless blue catfish, full size at left, may reach a hundred pounds or more. The broad, flat snout of the paddlefish possibly helps stabilize its body as it sieves with gaping jaw for crustaceans and plankton.

Prowling for food, shovelnose sturgeons rake mud near the bank with sensitive fleshy barbels that help the weak-eyed fish detect snails, crawfish, and insect larvae; they vacuum the morsels through tubelike mouths. Heavily ridged shells cover alligator snapping turtles. One lures six-inch green sunfish with wormlike "bait," an extension of the tongue. Breaking the surface of the river, another turtle startles a mallard into flight.

Confederate cannon crown a Mississippi bluff at Vicksburg National Military Park. On July 4, 1863, defenders surrendered the city after a 47-day siege. Vicksburg's fall gave the Union full control of the Mississippi and prompted President Lincoln to declare: "The Father of Waters again goes unvexed to the sea." Seventeen thousand Union soldiers lie in Vicksburg National Cemetery (right); the City Cemetery nearby holds uncounted thousands of Confederates. Ranger-historian Lloyd Clark (left) wears Confederate garb during cannon-firing demonstrations in the park.

Bound homeward after a day on the Vicksburg waterfront, a fisherman walks past the
Sprague, largest stern-wheel towboat ever built and now a bankside showboat and
museum. Put into service in 1903 and known as "Big Mama," the 318-foot vessel worked
until 1948. Today her "River Hall of Fame" displays scale models of river craft. In
1950 Hollywood moviemakers refurbished the big steamer for a role in "Show Boat."

COLLECTION OF MRS. GEORGE M. D. KELLY, NATCHEZ (ABOVE); PAINTING BY JOHN SYME, WHITE HOUSE COLLECTION (BELOW, CENTER); REDHEADED WOODPECKER

*"Most Romantick" Natchez,
Mississippi (above), painted
by John James Audubon
in the 1820's, occupies bluffs
overlooking the river. Audubon
traveled the Mississippi
in search of specimens
for his art. After shooting
creatures such as the redheaded woodpecker (left)
and the gray fox (right),
he positioned them on wires
to preserve a lifelike quality.*

*Once a cotton shipping port, the
ghost town of Rodney, Mississippi,
now lies neglected five miles east of
the river that brought it wealth. The
settlement fell into decay when the
capricious Mississippi began to shift
away from it in the 1870's. The porch
of the frame house above shades one
of the hundred or so residents. On the
main street another climbs astride a
mule. Downstream, inmates of the
Louisiana State Penitentiary at
Angola wrestle a steer to the ground.
The annual rodeo, open to the public,
supports the inmate welfare fund.*

Antebellum Rosedown at St. Francisville, Louisiana, mirrors the lifestyle of wealthy landowners whose plantations lined the Mississippi's banks from New Orleans to Natchez. Built in 1835 and restored in the 1960's as a showplace of the Old South, Rosedown exhibits European and American period furniture collected by the home's builders, Daniel and Martha Turnbull. The present owners opened the house to the public in 1964. A marble fountain gleams at dusk, and raindrops bead floribunda roses. Spanish moss drapes trees on the parklike grounds.

Storage tanks and operating towers of the Enjay Chemical Company (foreground) merge with those of the Humble Oil & Refining Company on the outskirts of Baton Rouge, Louisiana. Largest oil refinery in the United States, the Humble complex processes some 400,000 barrels of crude oil a day to make hundreds of products such as gasoline, jet fuel, kerosene, lubricating oils, industrial greases, waxes, and asphalt.

October sun burns away morning mist over Alligator Bayou in the Louisiana delta southeast of Baton Rouge

id cypresses festooned with Spanish moss, fishermen in johnboats cast for bass and bream.

ROM BATON ROUGE to the Gulf of Mexico the Mississippi's banks have echoed accents of many languages since the first European settlers arrived early in the 18th century. Flags of five nations, and those of the short-lived Republic of West Florida and the seceded Sovereign State of Louisiana, have flown over the bayou country.

Those early settlers—mostly French, German, and Spanish—fed their families with game and fish and the harvest from fertile gardens and small rice patches. But to prosper, they needed a cash crop. Efforts to grow indigo failed when crops were wiped out by disease and insects; tobacco grew in limited quantities. Finally, after the turn of the 19th century, they and the newly arrived Americans found the answer in sugarcane and then cotton. Later, in the 1880's, rice became a profitable prairie crop.

A rice expert named "Tiny" Grigsby walked with me along the levee below Baton Rouge, watching blackbirds winging home to the riverside forest from a day of raiding one of the few rice fields still remaining on the Mississippi bottomlands. For hours we had exchanged reminiscences: To my surprise the Dr. Reed Grigsby, rice marketing specialist at Louisiana State University toward whom rice dealers from Missouri south had steered me, turned out to be a man I remembered as "Tiny," a Navy roommate during World War II. When we settled down to business, he outlined the standing of the United States in the world rice market.

"With less than 2 percent of the world production, we furnished some 30 percent of the rice moved in international trade during the late 1960's. About half of America's rice grows in two states bordering the lower river —Arkansas and Louisiana. Both have long growing seasons, soil that holds water, and flat terrain that makes irrigating easy. In 1969 rice moved to the top of the list as Louisiana's most valuable crop, with cotton falling to fourth place after soybeans and sugarcane."

Priests planted Louisiana's first rice in 1718, and for a century and a half it was grown haphazardly along the bayous. Settlers called it "Providence rice"—there would be a crop if Providence sent the right conditions.

Large-scale production of rice came with the settling of the southwestern Louisiana prairies after a railroad reached there from New Orleans in 1882. The world market was waiting, and today 74 percent of the Louisiana rice crop goes out to sea.

But it was sugar, not rice, that supported an extravagant slave-based way of life for Creole planters. The first crop in 1751 went mostly into rum.

But in 1795 Etienne de Boré showed how to granulate sugar from cane juice, and an immensely profitable industry was born.

Today, however, riverbank sugarcane fields are in demand for industrial sites. Denver T. Loupe, sugarcane specialist at Louisiana State University in Baton Rouge, is disturbed by the trend: "The 1971 Louisiana crop will grow on 330,000 acres yielding some 4,600 pounds per acre. About 35 percent of the acreage is still on the banks of the Mississippi, but in the past ten years, industry has built riverside plants that have taken 10,000 acres of prime sugarcane land out of production. I can foresee industry's driving sugar entirely from the river's banks. Most of it now is grown along the Lafourche and Teche bayous.

"Yet a 15 percent restoration in the Government's acreage allotment for St. James Parish, one of our most highly industrialized areas, would mean 2,000 acres and an annual gross of as much as a million dollars if the acreage were prime riverbank land. Suppose an industry with that kind of payroll came to St. James—it would make headlines.

"Of course, industries can make immediate payment of $2,000 to $5,000 an acre for river frontage, and many of them need to be directly on the river for water supply and for docks. But some types of related industries could use inferior land back from the river just as well. One day we may very well wish we had not sold all those fertile riverbanks."

I recalled those blackbirds Tiny and I had watched returning from their banquet in the riverbank rice fields. Sometimes they become a staple themselves for a lower river delight called jambalaya.

After the French Canadian farmers of Acadia—now Nova Scotia—were scattered by the British 20 years before the American Revolution, they began to recongregate in Louisiana in the 1760's and 1780's. There they took game and shellfish from the teeming forests, bayous, and marshes and, like the Creoles, added rice, blending it all with Indian, Spanish, and African seasonings to create a distinctive cuisine. In time Acadians became Cajuns, with jambalaya their most famous dish.

Any kind of meat can be used except fish, which is too soft. Individual recipes call for birds or wild game, from blackbirds or doves to squirrels or deer; or for chicken—best for a large quantity because it's inexpensive—ham, pork, crawfish, crabs, shrimp, or some combination of them.

At Gonzales, about 25 miles south of Baton Rouge and four miles beyond the industrial strip along the river, Chief Deputy Sheriff John D. Gonzales guided me around the two-day Jambalaya Festival. At this annual affair a dozen or so men—those most in demand as jambalaya cooks at church fairs, political rallies, and big family celebrations—compete for the world championship. They cook enough jambalaya to serve the whole crowd, and that meant, when I was there, 11,000 servings at a dollar a plate.

Over smoking wood fires laid on the bare ground, chicken, seasonings, and rice simmered in closed cast-iron washpots, many of them generations old and most holding 18 to 30 gallons.

At one side, John Hebert of Arnaudville played an accordion accompaniment for a quartet of Cajuns roaring a rollicking, beery concert of "Jolie Blonde," "Calinda," "Fais Poto Cayette," and "Jambalaya."

Among the judges were a sports editor, a district judge, and a mayor. They solemnly tasted each numbered sample, cleared their palates with Beaujolais, and proceeded to the next dish.

Donnie D. Mire, a 38-year-old worker at a nearby alumina extracting plant and a practiced jambalaya cook, sidled up and informed me out of the corner of his mouth that the whole sampling was a waste of time, for his dish was a sure winner. As it turned out, he was right; and he won not only a two-quart silver replica of a Cajun cook pot but also the use of a new car for a year, thanks to a jambalaya-loving Gonzales dealer.

Donnie gave me his recipe for serving a hundred people, but I was even more impressed after persuading Gil Braud to write out his for my wife's instruction. He mixes 800 pounds of chicken with 400 pounds of rice and 200 pounds of onions, a seven-pound pinch of salt, a three-pound dash of black pepper, 12 bottles of Tabasco, a bushel of green peppers, and a pound of garlic. He cooks in a huge old syrup kettle, and serves more than "1,000 visitors or 100 hungry Cajuns, whichever get there first."

Deputy Gonzales hovered over the bubbling pots until the cooking was done; then he chose four at random, put them in the back of a pickup truck, and sped toward New Orleans 60 miles away. There the annual Food Festival was under way, and its officials were determined that the superb upriver Cajun jambalaya should be served at their event. Police motorcycles were waiting at the city limits to escort 80 gallons of jambalaya to Rivergate Center.

I followed at a more leisurely pace, and began a round of some of the world's great restaurants. New Orleans takes its gastronomy seriously, and its distinguished eating places range from a hotel dining room—the Pontchartrain—to some tiny, highly informal retreats.

For a real Cajun blend of roux and rice, crawfish and crab, I dined at the Bon Ton Cafe, a cozy place on Magazine Street, not in the French Quarter. It is fitted like a Parisian bistro with exposed-beam ceilings, hurricane lamps, and red and white checkered tablecloths. Owner Alvin P. Pierce, an old friend, speaks with the Cajun accents of his boyhood home on Bayou Lafourche, and cooks only family recipes. He keeps a reasonably varied cellar, but he has discovered a happy affinity between Vouvray white— still or sparkling—and the shellfish dishes that distinguish the Cajun cook. So Vouvray white I drank, to grace red snapper throats, crawfish bisque, and a platter of buster crabs cooked in their own fat. A true Cajun son of the lowlands, Alvin has developed his cuisine from foods available to the humblest bayou dweller, the yield of marsh and seacoast.

Though Creole French culture does not pervade the city as it did before the Civil War, the Gallic presence remains, and the French Quarter, or Vieux Carré—Old Square—commands the interest of visitors. At Flag Day ceremonies in Jackson Square, the band improvised unprogrammed and nostalgic notes from "La Marseillaise" to interrupt the otherwise all-American patriotic proceedings. In the garden behind St. Louis Cathedral and adjacent to Père Antoine's Alley, I spied a coffeepot and joined a group of ladies and priests for a Sunday-morning chat in French. The very parking meters of the Quarter tell you in careful detail in French how to insert a nickel to get 15 minutes *pour cinq sous.*

The French flag fluttered to earth in that same square on December 20, 1803, and the American flag rose, signaling transfer of the vast Louisiana Territory. Soon a flood of English-speaking immigrants began to pour into New Orleans from the Atlantic seaboard and upper Mississippi Valley; after the War of 1812, climaxed by Andrew Jackson's victory below New Orleans in January 1815, the influx increased.

The Creoles, proud of their French and Spanish heritage, clung to their ancestral homes in the Quarter as a bastion of French-speaking warmth and chivalry threatened by the ambitious, aggressive newcomers. The Americans, or "Bostonais," settled across Canal Street and, as they prospered, built palatial houses that still stand as monuments to their business acumen. They surrounded the houses with plantings, and that area became known as the Garden District. The heat and rain of summer and the fogs of a mild winter fostered among the great oaks a luxuriant growth of palms, dense subtropical ground covers, camellias, and azaleas.

Summer tourists in New Orleans join the residents in their gratitude for air conditioning, as much for its humidity control as for its defense against the heat. Winter visitors seldom wear overcoats—they need protection from frost only three or four times a year. A severe freeze is so rare that water pipes are still put on the outside of buildings. The same climate that stimulates magnificent gardens and flowering patios encourages mold and dry rot, so builders use resistant cypress and specially formulated paints. Maintenance is obviously important; neglected houses rapidly become sagging ruins overgrown by tangles of vines and weeds.

New Orleans flourishes as a vacationists' destination not because of climate but because, in various ways, it evokes pleasure, nostalgia, excitement. Its historic streets and buildings, its famed wrought-iron balconies, its gardens, its food, its music all contribute; but nothing demonstrates better the importance New Orleans places on *joie de vivre*—joy of living extended in this case to the carefree foolishness of childhood—than the pre-Lenten carnival season crowned by Mardi Gras, "Fat Tuesday."

This midwinter whirl of parties, parades, impromptu jazz concerts on street corners, costume balls open only to insiders—but so numerous that almost anybody can become an insider with some group or other—all culminates in licensed lunacy on the last day before Lent's austerities begin on Ash Wednesday. The celebration evolved solely for the amusement of New Orleans residents, not for that of outsiders; but it has become the city's major tourist attraction, and hundreds of thousands of visitors flock there every year to join in the merriment.

Carnival starts with Twelfth Night and ends with Shrove Tuesday, but it is a major year-round industry. In warehouses scattered about the city and the surrounding countryside, designers and artisans create fantasies in floats and ballroom scenery for next year's events. The yellow pages of the telephone directory list a dozen companies specializing in floats and holiday decorations, and hundreds of others count carnival costumes, decorations, and souvenirs as important parts of their business.

Like thousands of fellow citizens along the Mississippi's southern reaches, I consider New Orleans the capital of my region. I go there after a long stretch of work to refresh my senses. Its heady perfume is compounded of the fragrances of flowering plants, fermenting beer, and bubbling caldrons of crabs seasoned with peppercorns. Its flavors are those of many cuisines but especially Creole. Above all I savor the sharpness of coffee chicory-enriched and double-dripped to make a tar-colored brew that leaves a stain on the cup and an equal imprint on the memory.

Some publicists persist in calling the city the "Paris of North America." But even the French Quarter appears only distantly related to the Gallic mother city. Its lush courtyards, the lacy iron grillwork and plastered façades, the balconies sheltering strollers from frequent showers, the shady patios, the banana leaves flapping in soft breezes—these come straight from the tropical seas just beyond the river's mouth. Yet the European overtones are unmistakable, and New Orleans somehow suggests all at once America, Europe, and the Caribbean.

And its nighttime streets sound somewhat like a blend of the Caribbean and Africa, yet distinctively like themselves—for this is the very birthplace of American jazz.

Visitors hear New Orleans jazz mostly on Bourbon Street and in nearby parts of the old city. Except for the musicians at determinedly unpretentious Preservation Hall and a few similar locations, most of the Quarter's modern jazzmen have taken on a polish foreign to the music's origins. But nearby, out of sight of most tourists, the roots of the Afro-American folk music that became jazz live on.

Across the river in Gretna one steaming Sunday morning, I met in a shopping-center parking lot with the Tuxedo Brass Band. Trumpets and trombones, saxophones and drums blared a Dixieland number as we led a Sunday-school parade two miles to the New Hope Baptist Church, where the West Side Baptist Missionary Association was holding its 38th annual session. Along the way, I struck up a shouted conversation with Andrew Morgan, leader of the Tuxedos and a kind of elder statesman of the marching bands, best known for their performances in funeral processions.

"This morning at breakfast the young men was gobbling eggs like chickens have give up laying," Mr. Morgan said into my ear. "Thinking about this hot sun, I told them not to let their mouths give their feet a bad time. We got a long walk ahead."

Mr. Morgan carried an umbrella, as did at least half the marchers. In several cases this apparently traditional accessory of the jazz walker had a purely symbolic function, for some of the younger people held aloft umbrella handles topped by ribs totally innocent of cloth covering — although some were gaily decorated with feathers, tassels, and even Kewpie dolls. But Mr. Morgan's purpose was practical: "I always got my umbrella with me," he said. "In New Orleans, if it ain't raining, the sun is blazing down, and anyhow it's always handy in case it comes up a fight."

A woman from a rival congregation came to the steps of her church to protest the noise as we passed. With impeccable courtesy, Mr. Morgan doffed his hat and bowed. "The Good Book say make a joyful noise unto the Lord, Madam, and that what we doin'."

The band marched on to "Walking with the King."

The river winds another hundred miles to reach the Gulf, yet the sea dominates the city. On the waterfront at Jackson Square a concrete floodwall screens the view of bustling traffic on the Mississippi, but visitors who climb the ramp to the floodwall opening can stand on a long promenade there and watch a steady parade of freighters, finding among them the flags of almost all the maritime nations of the world. Tugs chuff about busily, and their cousins, the bluff-bowed towboats, push rafts of barges between industrial wharves.

Riprap protects the levee from waters pounding across Algiers Bend. At this extremely sharp, difficult curve and again at Gouldsboro Bend just upstream, stop-and-go lights control boat traffic when the river is rising or falling rapidly. The levees are particularly essential to New Orleans, for much of it is below sea level. But while keeping the river out they keep the rainfall in, so an elaborate pumping system takes rainwater over the levees and into the city's huge Lake Pontchartrain, which opens to the sea.

Out of sight behind more levees on the outskirts of town lie immense industrial plants dependent on the river-sea complex of shipping and the vast supply of fresh water offered by the Mississippi.

In tonnage and in dollar value of exports New Orleans ranks as second port of the United States, next to New York City. Port-related activities bring in 72 cents of every dollar of New Orleans income. More than a million metropolitan residents go to sleep to the sounds of seagoing ships.

At his office in New Orleans, I talked with Jerome L. Goldman, designer of a line of ships coupling river barge shipment with overseas trade. Labeled LASH vessels — for Lighter Aboard Ship — the 859-foot freighters carry cranes for hoisting special river barges, or lighters, aboard. Filled with cargo, the barges weigh up to a million pounds each. The cranes can stack them four deep in the hold and two deep on deck, up to a total of 80.

"When a LASH ship arrives at an overseas port, the ship's crane lifts the barges out and onto the water. River tugs or towboats push the shallow-draft barges, tied together into rafts, to inland destinations," Mr. Goldman said. "LASH vessels make ocean ports of cities like Knoxville, on the Tennessee River, Wheeling, West Virginia, on the Ohio, and even Catoosa, Oklahoma, Tulsa's port on the Arkansas-Verdigris River system. One large LASH ship could serve a whole archipelago having only shallow ports, such as Indonesia, from one central point where barges would be picked up by inter-island feeder vessels. Right now, the *Acadia Forest* drops barges at Rotterdam for movement up the Rhine as far inland as Switzerland."

At the time Mr. Goldman and I talked, four LASH ships were in service and more were under construction, 11 of them at Avondale Shipyards, nine miles upriver from New Orleans and the largest commercial shipbuilder in the United States. Mr. Goldman expects a hundred LASH vessels to be afloat by 1975.

I went upriver past the Huey Long Bridge — a reminder of Louisiana's colorful, audacious governor and senator who was assassinated in 1935 — to visit Avondale. There I saw work proceeding not only on LASH ships but also on another vessel of special interest to me: the U.S.S. *Blakely*, a Knox-class destroyer-escort. The little "tin cans" I conned during World War II carried a smidgeon of every kind of armament to fit them for varied and unpredictable duties. The *Blakely* had been stripped of almost all defensive weapons except for a single cannon, but a rocket launcher and four torpedo tubes gave it formidable weaponry against submarines.

Almost as revolutionary as the LASH concept is that of the containerized ships — small ones like the miniships that go upriver to Greenville, and huge freighters that haul hundreds of metal boxes the size of transport truck trailers. Such cargo containers ride to and from wharves by truck or rail. With one lift of the crane, thousands of pounds go aboard ship. One crane can move as many as 20 containers an hour.

Transport trucks need space to maneuver, and containers need storage space, so Centroport U.S.A. was designed. Now under construction in the heart of a new industrial area on the east side of the city, it connects with the river by a canal and navigation lock. The new port lies at the head of a deep-draft channel, the Mississippi River-Gulf Outlet, constructed by the Corps of Engineers and opened to traffic in 1963. It makes a shortcut across the marshes to the Gulf 76 miles away and connects to the eastern half of the Intracoastal Waterway, reaching to northern Florida. The first wharves, with machinery to lift and move containerized cargo, will be ready for business by 1972.

Verdun Daste, of the New Orleans Port Commission, toured the port area with me. He said the Commission predicts that by the year 2000 many New Orleans wharves will have moved from the river to the Mississippi River-Gulf Outlet, clearing some 11 miles of the present 13-mile port area along the city waterfront for other purposes: hotels, parks, playgrounds, passenger-ship terminals.

"Container ships need five to ten acres of marshaling yards behind every dock," he said. "Older wharves on the New Orleans riverfront lack the necessary back-up space for the assembly of cargo."

Of the nearly 5,000 ships that come into New Orleans each year, almost all continue to use the Mississippi River channel, which leads directly into the present terminals. Only a few hundred come through the seaway, mostly bulk carriers heading for new bulk terminals not far from the containerized wharves. "But more and more ships will use the seaway as new facilities on it are added," Verdun said.

That night I toured waterfront hangouts and met some of the sailors who bring those ships to port. At the Acropolis on Decatur Street, facing the river, crews of several Greek ships competed at dancing to *bouzouki* music vibrating out of a Greek-only jukebox. Grace and precision dominated until midnight. Then a young Greek with the chest and forearms of a colossus rose above those niceties. He gripped the corner of a table between his teeth, straightened up without the help of his hands, and danced a ponderous tour of the room, the table held horizontally rigid in his jaws. He spilled not a drop of beer from the glasses on the table. The thunderous applause brought an encore: He grabbed the back of a chair between his teeth and, without using either hand, tilted it upright over his head to make another circle of the room, staying scrupulously in time with the beat.

I spent the next day in the air, flying down to the Gulf and then over the birdfoot delta in a plane piloted by Allan B. Ensminger, chief of the Refuge Division, Louisiana Wildlife and Fisheries Commission. In 1965 Al had piloted me on a flight to assess damage after Hurricane Betsy. This time we had a sadly similar mission: to survey the extent of recovery from the crushing blows of Hurricane Camille in 1969, the most ferocious storm to hit North America in man's memory.

The marsh areas south of Venice, Louisiana, last solid ground along the channel to the sea, are ideal habitats for the hundreds of thousands of migratory wildfowl that winter there. A large part of the Delta National Wildlife Refuge, the adjacent Pass a Loutre Refuge, and a privately owned area of comparable size on the river's west bank suffered severe damage.

As we flew over the vast marshes—monotonously dun-colored now in winter, but various shades of green, yellow-green, and red in other seasons—we looked for some of the 900 deer that once roamed here. We saw a single survivor who tried to hide from us behind the only tree for miles, a scrawny willow. Al told me he had counted several dozen deer, enough to refill in time the ecological vacuum; but the great herd that once occupied the grassy wilderness perished on the night of the big wind.

Alligators sunned themselves everywhere, it seemed, and I remarked that I had thought them to be on the edge of extinction.

"They were, five or six years ago," Al said, "and paradoxically that's why you see so many little ones. Once everybody became alarmed enough to protect them truly—a state law made it illegal to kill them—they started a comeback almost overnight. We now have 300,000 or more, easily, and once they reach the point of overpopulation they'll begin cannibalizing the babies—as they've already started doing in one pocket in western Louisiana. So someday we might even have a limited season. Right now, though, with a new Federal law making it an offense to ship illegally taken alligator skins across state lines, it's useless effort for a poacher to drag 150 pounds of dead 'gator out of the marsh."

Swinging low over sandbars and islands awash in the shallow transition zone between fresh and brackish waters, Al pointed out dark streaks of oil drifting toward refuge grasslands and rich oyster reefs just north.

"Everybody gets upset about the massive but rare oil-rig fires—there've been fewer than half a dozen altogether—but the bootleg pumping of oil waste from rigs has a far greater effect on wildlife: waterfowl, shrimp and oysters, and fur-bearing animals like the nutria and muskrat that make trapping an important industry here," he said.

As far as oysters are concerned, it's actually better when the oil slick stays on top of the water, I learned. If the oil gets mixed into the column of water the oyster is pumping in and out of its system, it makes it taste like a garage mechanic's oily rag. Eventually, clean water will purge it. But if enough oil sinks down onto the baby oysters, they may suffocate.

"In those state-maintained reefs down there east of the river," Al said, "about 80 percent of Louisiana's seed oysters are grown to be given free to oyster farmers, whose beds are mostly west of the river or north of the Delta Refuge." He added that Louisiana harvests 25 percent of all the oysters and shrimp produced in the United States.

"The biggest effect of all on this habitat comes not from oil but from those faint, watery lines crisscrossing the marshes," Al said. "They're canals made during exploration for oil, or access channels to oil equipment. Wherever they're cut, seawater intrudes and drives out or kills off many of the marsh and marine creatures that had been living there and starts a rapid erosion of the river-built delta."

We swung back toward New Orleans. In the dusk, burning gas flares and lights on hundreds of offshore oil rigs and platforms rivaled the glow of the city. From those wells comes an eighth of the Nation's oil—and from the waters they stand in, about 40 percent of the commercial fish catch.

I boarded the *M/V King Aegeus* one morning at the invitation of Captain George Damalas, a young man from the Greek island of Khíos. Bound for Constanţa, Rumania, on the Black Sea, Captain Damalas carried a cargo of fabricated steel. Over a glass of ouzo in his cabin, he spoke of the long absences from home: "We stay out 12 to 14 months at a time. Every sailor gets 20 days' annual paid vacation, but most become so lonesome at sea that they stay ashore three or four months out of their own pocket."

We mounted to the bridge and met Captain Carl L. Dietze, Jr., our pilot for the run to Pilottown. He got us under way—in Greek.

"*Déxiá*," he said, and the helmsman turned the big freighter to starboard. "*Méssi*," and the helm came amidships. "*Grámmi*," and we steadied on the course. I expressed my admiration for his learning.

"After 20 years, I'd be pretty stupid if I didn't know the commands in all the languages," he replied. "You need only about six words in each to get the ship to Pilottown. I can't even order a ham sandwich in Greek."

We moved past the entrance to Harvey Canal, connecting link to Barataria Bayou and the western half of the Intracoastal Waterway going all the way to Brownsville, Texas. Sixty miles south of New Orleans, we passed Port Sulphur on the west bank. Nearly a dozen mini-mountains of sulphur rose 40 feet above the flat landscape. Most of Freeport Minerals Company's production from four nearby mines is delivered by ship and tank barge as hot liquid, but about 10 percent is stored here in solid form. The liquid sulphur is pumped into shallow vats 200 feet wide and 250 feet long. When it hardens, the metal rims of the vats are raised and more layers are added.

To ship the dry sulphur, a large scoop digs into the block and transfers a load to a crusher; the broken material, resembling yellow gravel, is then carried by ship to chemical plants in Florida and foreign ports and by barge throughout the Mississippi Valley's river system.

When we reached Pilottown, Captain Leon C. Buras, Jr., the bar pilot, came aboard to relieve Captain Dietze. He would take us to the Head of Passes two miles south, then out South Pass another 13½ miles to the Gulf. We pressed on through the night, with the low-lying shores—now narrowing strips of marsh—barely visible; at intervals navigation lights shone steadily or blinked in sequence. Beyond them, in the water, quick-flashing white lights on oil wells and platforms dotted the darkness. Captain Buras peered out intently though he knew every navigation light by heart. Suddenly an inbound Danish motor vessel approached, and it seemed to me that it was heading straight for us and would run us into the marsh. But each pilot, following the rule of the road, kept to his right, and we passed in the channel as closely as two automobiles meeting on a narrow two-lane highway.

At the Head of Passes the river splits into three main channels to the sea—Pass a Loutre, South Pass, and Southwest Pass. All major shipping uses either South Pass, 30 feet deep, or Southwest Pass, 40 feet.

During the 19th century, shoals at the Head of Passes and sand and mysterious mud lumps at the river mouths threatened to close one of the world's mightiest waterways to seagoing traffic, for dredges could not keep up in their contest with river and tides. Finally only small vessels of very shallow draft could cross from the open sea to the river during low tide, and even at high water large ships had to be towed over the sandbars.

In 1875 James B. Eads, the civil engineer who had bridged the river at St. Louis, received approval from Congress to try a daring concept: a jetty system to make the Mississippi cut and scour its own channel through South Pass. It was an unconventional agreement because Eads, through a public company, would finance the construction till he had secured a channel depth of 20 feet; even then he would receive only a partial payment; additional installments would depend not only on depth reached but also on the effectiveness of the jetty system over an extended period.

Although handicapped throughout the project by disputes with Government officials and the Corps of Engineers, Eads persisted—and was brilliantly successful. With a loyal crew of about 75 men, he built two parallel walls of pilings, willow mattresses, and rubble, capped by enormous concrete blocks, to create a passage less than a quarter of a mile wide out to the deep waters of the Gulf. In only 15 months the 20-foot depth was a reality, and he could write that "the largest coastal steamers trading in New Orleans have been sent to sea over the bar on which scarcely eight feet of water could be found last year." By 1879 the 30-foot depth was achieved and the jetty system completed. It was a great bargain for the Government, for the total was only $5,250,000, about half the cost of a proposed canal.

Traveling down the pass that Eads created, we reached the sea buoy beyond the coastal shallows shortly after midnight, and Captain Buras turned the vessel over to Captain Damalas for the 21-day haul to Constanţa. We boarded the pilot boat and returned to Port Eads, the pilots' station on the extreme tip of narrow land behind the jetty.

In six months I had come from a snack at the Headwaters Inn, the first house on the river below Lake Itasca, to a plate of cold beans, fried eggs, and canned peppers with the pilots at the last house on the river.

Next day I flew back to New Orleans and rode up to the revolving bar-lounge atop the International Trade Mart. As the glow of the western sky faded, the city lights twinkled on. Automobiles crept across the Greater New Orleans Bridge toward the west-bank suburbs, meeting another line of cars carrying their passengers into New Orleans for a night of pleasure. On the river below, tugboats hurried on errands for tramp steamers. In the twilight I could still make out the flags of Yugoslavia, Korea, Norway, Japan, and Greece. At the marshaling yards a wealth of products from half the continental United States awaited shipment to distant shores.

Everybody up and down the river is sure he understands his little piece of it. But few comprehend its immense importance to America and the world till they have looked on that bustling congress of ships assembled from the corners of the earth to gather the riches of the lands drained by the mighty Mississippi.

First black Louisiana legislator elected in the 20th century, Ernest N. "Dutch" Morial, with a young friend, Brian Hall, answers the telephone during a visit at Thugs United, Inc., only city-wide ghetto youth organization in New Orleans.

Laying down a mattress of concrete, men and machines labor to contain the Mississippi. Slabs linked together with steel cables slide off the sloping deck of a launching boat near Reserve, Louisiana, to form an underwater revetment that will keep the current's destructive forces from eroding the riverbank. At right, a crane lowers a section into position for linkup. Perspiration beads a worker's face (left).

179

Cook Gil Braud (above, wearing straw hat) and assistant Wilbur Austen stir a steaming pot of jambalaya—chicken, rice, onions, and seasonings—at the 1970 Jambalaya Festival in Gonzales, Louisiana. French Canadian farmers, uprooted by the British, adopted jambalaya from earlier Creole settlers, making it with birds, wild game, shellfish, or chicken, as well as pork. At right, Miss Jambalaya, Lynn Mayon, joins a crowd of merrymakers pressing close to hear accordionist John Hebert squeeze out traditional Cajun tunes; Mr. and Mrs. Sitman Loupe enjoy a street dance at the festival.

DAVID R. BRIDGE, N.G.S. STAFF (BELOW); N.G.S. PHOTOGRAPHER JAMES L. STANFIELD

Held to its course by earthen levees, the Mississippi sweeps past New Orleans, where some streets lie five feet below sea level. The port stands second in the Nation—after New York—in tonnage and value of foreign commerce; an average of more than one ship every two hours docks there. One river curve inspired a nickname for the metropolis: the Crescent City. On the horizon stretches 621-square-mile Lake Pontchartrain.

Towers of St. Louis Cathedral loom over Jackson Square in New Orleans'
French Quarter, site of the original city. Nearby, the French Market
displays plump watermelons and strings of garlic. Across town,
the St. Charles Street trolley (above) clanks through gathering dusk.

Dancing to the beat, Chris Owens belts out a song at the 809 Club on Bourbon Street. Long famous for night life blended in varying proportions of sin and sophistication, the French Quarter by day holds different charms for artist and visitor alike. A pigeon balances precariously on the outstretched hand of a boy in Jackson Square; the United States flag first flew there in 1803 after the Louisiana Purchase. Artist Bill Christian (opposite left) paints typical Quarter scenes; nearby, a sari-clad Pakistani poses for another artist.

Trumpeter Kid Thomas Valentine and his band set hands clapping in time to traditional jazz at Preservation Hall, a living museum in the French Quarter. Some of the men
who helped create jazz in the early 20th century in New Orleans play there nightly.
Patrons each drop a dollar into a basket at the door. At far left, Grand Marshal
Matthew "Fats" Houston leads the procession for the jazz funeral of clarinetist Emile
Barnes. Outside the cemetery after the burial, drummer Henry "Booker T." Glass
breaks into a smile as Dejan's Olympia Brass Band swings from dirges to jazz.

Overleaf: Parade honoring Rex, King of Carnival, navigates a sea of humanity overflowing 170-foot-wide Canal Street on Shrove Tuesday, last day of revelry before Lent.
From the floats, costumed riders toss Mardi Gras "doubloons"—prized souvenirs.

DAVID R. BRIDGE, N.G.S. STAFF (BELOW); N.G.S. PHOTOGRAPHER JAMES L. STANFIELD

Lookout at Southwest Pass Bar Pilot Station, last outpost on the Mississippi, scans the horizon for approaching ocean vessels. The U. S. Coast Guard lighthouse (right) overlooks South Pass, the other major shipping route to the Gulf of Mexico. Bar pilots steer ships through the narrow channels to Pilottown, where river pilots take over for the 90 miles north to New Orleans. Just south of there, a tugboat helps guide the Elizabeth Lykes *(left) past other freighters waiting their turn at the docks.*

Screaming gulls ride the wind above a trawler bound homeward after a night of fishing for shrimp in the Gulf. Approaching Southwest Pass, major shipping channel through the delta, she bucks the outpouring current of the mighty Mississippi, a force that has gathered strength from watersheds in two Canadian provinces and 31 states.

Index

Illustrations references appear in *italics*.

Composition for *The Mighty Mississippi* by National Geographic's Phototypographic Division, John E. McConnell, Manager. Printed and bound by Fawcett Printing Corp., Rockville, Md. Color separations by Beck Engraving Company, Philadelphia, Pa., Colorgraphics, Inc., Beltsville, Md., Graphic Color Plate, Inc., Stamford, Conn., The Lanman Company, Alexandria, Va., Lebanon Valley Offset Company, Inc., Annville, Pa., McCall Printing Company, Charlotte, N.C., Progressive Color Corp., Rockville, Md., and Stevenson Photocolor, Inc., Cincinnati, Ohio.

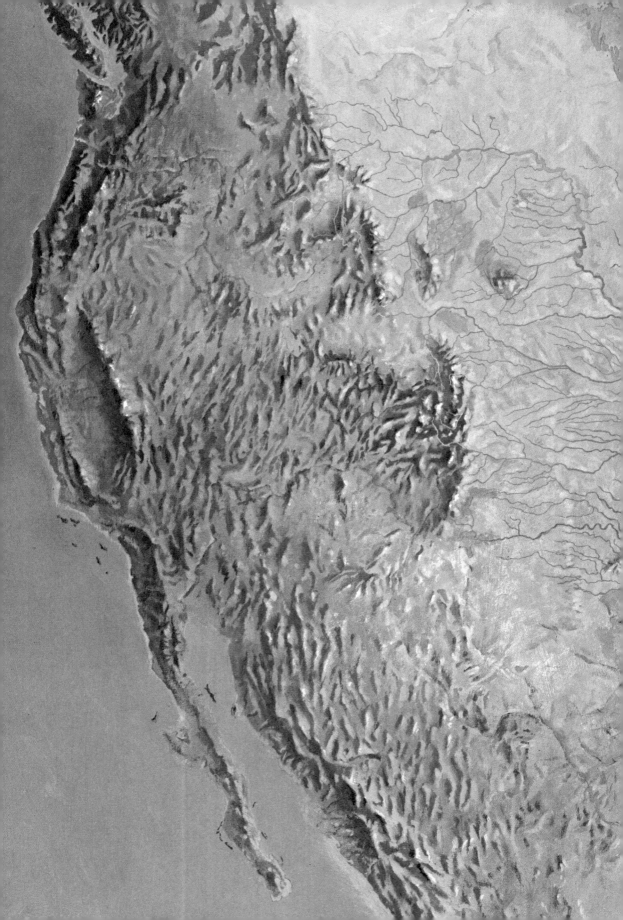